To my "friend" Joe,

May each of us have
such multiple friends in our
lives and such blessings and
graces to recognize the plan for each
of them in our journey.

Y'ls Joann
2/07

Praise for ONE YARD SHORT

"In life we would all prefer victories, but many times God uses setbacks and apparent defeats to build our character, strengthen our faith, and set us squarely on His path. In *One Yard Short*, 32-year coaching veteran Les Steckel takes his reader inside the world of competitive sports and shows how God used adversity to advance him into true victory."

—Dr. Charles F. Stanley, Pastor of First Baptist Atlanta
and president of In Touch Ministries

"Our victories and losses may not be as public as NFL and college coach Les Steckel has experienced, but what God taught him in some painful losses will encourage everyone who reads *One Yard Short*."

—Joe Gibbs, NFL Hall of Fame,
head coach of the Washington Redskins

"Football parallels a lot of what life offers us. Sometimes our forward progress is stopped short of our goals. From his many years of college and NFL coaching, Les describes sound principles to live by and confirms that life's greatest victories often come after embarrassing defeats."

—Raymond Berry, NFL Hall of Fame player and
former head coach of the New England Patriots

"'Upon further review,' your losses may actually propel you toward your most gratifying victories. Read how game loss, job loss, and genuine brokenness for Coach Steckel ultimately enabled him to experience victory he could only have dreamed about."

—Grant Teaff, Executive Director,
American Football Coaches Association

"All of us have at one time or another come up 'One Yard Short' on some project we attempted. Frustration, embarrassment, bitterness—these things are common responses to our losses. Learn from long-time NFL coach Les Steckel that your most satisfying victories in life may be an outcome of your worst and most painful defeats."

—Bill McCartney, Former head football coach at the
University of Colorado, and founder of Promise Keepers

"*One Yard Short* is a compelling, real-life story. Coach Steckel's NFL experiences reflect life's victories and defeats. In Les' playbook each snap of the ball is designed for success. Each of us has much to learn from our own personal 'One Yard Short' experiences. This book reminds us that life is a journey, and that God has a plan for our destination."

—Ed T. Rush, Former director of officiating of the NBA

One Yard Short is much more than the story of one of pro football's most memorable games. It is an amazing story of perseverance under adversity, and a testimony to how all of our defeats can be turned into true victories.

—Kyle Rote, Jr., founder of
Athletic Resource Management, Inc.

Arguably the greatest play in Super Bowl history brought heart-wrenching defeat to the Tennessee Titans, and yet a new life mission for Coach Les Steckel. Man or woman, football fan or not, in *One Yard Short*, you'll gain amazing insights into lessons learned from sport's most competitive arena.

—Joe White, president of Kanakuk Kamps
and founder of Kids Across America

We all prefer victories, but Coach Steckel's life demonstrates that often we can learn more about ourselves and how God made us after devastating defeats. Reading *One Yard Short* will cause you to consider how you can turn your own disappointments into incredible opportunities.

—Alicia Landry, wife of Hall of Fame coach Tom Landry,
head coach of the Dallas Cowboys, 1960-1988

In *One Yard Short*, my friend Les Steckel draws from his extensive background as an NFL coach to challenge and teach lessons on life and faith that will equip and encourage readers to turn their defeats into victories. This is a book of hope for those who feel they have fallen short of their goals.

—Dr. Tony Evans, senior pastor of Oak Cliff Bible Fellowship,
Dallas, Texas, and founder of The Urban Alternative

"I have often said that competitive greatness is not about winning a game. It's about learning to give all we have to give. When we rise to every occasion, give our best effort and make those around us better, it ultimately does not matter if we are one basket (or one yard) short. As a player, and now as a mentor, Les Steckel truly embodies this principle. I have long supported the Fellowship of Christian Athletes and appreciated Les Steckel. Thank you, Les, for continuing to be a model for today's rising generation of young athletes."

—John Wooden, Basketball Hall of Fame player and coach

"On the football field you experience tremendous victories and great disappointments. In *One Yard Short*, Les Steckel talks about how to handle both—by keeping your eyes on God and letting Him direct you. Whether you are an athlete or not, you'll enjoy this book because it takes the lessons learned on the football field and applies them to the bigger game of life."

—Tony Dungy, Head coach of the Indianapolis Colts

ONE YARD
SHORT

TURNING YOUR DEFEATS INTO VICTORIES

LES STECKEL
with ROB SUGGS

W PUBLISHING GROUP
A Division of Thomas Nelson Publishers
Since 1798

www.wpublishinggroup.com

ONE YARD SHORT

Published by W Publishing Group, a division of Thomas Nelson, Inc., P.O. Box 141000, Nashville, Tennessee 37214.

W Publishing Group books may be purchased in bulk for educational, business, fund-raising, or sales promotional use. For information, please e-mail SpecialMarkets@ThomasNelson.com.

All Scripture quotations, unless otherwise indicated, are taken from the *Holy Bible*, New Living Translation, copyright © 1996. Used by permission of Tyndale House Publishers, Inc., Wheaton, Illinois 60189. All rights reserved.

Other Scripture references are from the following sources:

The Living Bible (TLB), copyright © 1971. Used by permission of Tyndale House Publishers, Inc., Wheaton, Illionis 60189. All rights reserved.

The Holy Bible, New International Version (NIV). Copyright © 1973, 1978, 1984 by International Bible Society. Used by permission of Zondervan. All rights reserved.

Library of Congress Cataloging-in-Publication Data

Steckel, Les, 1946-
   One yard short : turning your defeats into victories / Les Steckel, with Rob Suggs.
      p. cm.
   ISBN 10: 0-8499-0019-0 (Hard Cover)
   ISBN 13: 978-0-8499-0019-8 (Hard Cover)
   ISBN 10: 0-8499-9148-X (Special Edition)
   1. Steckel, Les, 1946- 2. Football coaches–United States–Biography.
I. Suggs, Rob. II. Title.
GV939.S735S84 2006
796.332092–dc22
[B]
2006012960

Printed in the United States of America
06 07 08 09 10 QWM 9 8 7 6 5 4 3 2

To my greatest teammates
Chris, Christian, Lesley, and Luke.
I will always love you and respect you.
You have richly blessed my life.

CONTENTS

1

Miracle in Music City

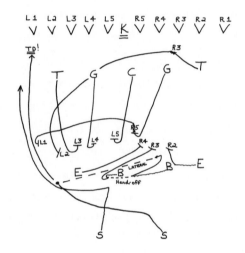

It's going to take a miracle for the Titans to pull this one out!"

The TV color commentator had it right. This game seemed as if it was all over but the shouting—and the Buffalo Bills were doing plenty of that. They were dancing, hugging, and celebrating wildly, and why not? For them, the miracle had already come: a 41-yard field goal to give them a 16–15 lead with only sixteen seconds left on the clock. All the Bills needed was one safe, well-placed kickoff, and they'd be on their way to the next round in the playoffs, perhaps ultimately the Super Bowl. We, the Tennessee Titans, would be on our way home. Done.

The date was January 8, 2000. As the Titans' offensive coordinator, I watched these waning moments from above the field, in the press box. I felt exhausted and devastated. After a long career in the NFL, I knew what it meant to fall short in a big game. But this one—well, this one was the most agonizing end to a season I could imagine. The football life is all about sacrifice. Had the sacrifice been worthwhile?

Here we were, 13–3 with a perfect record at home, Super Bowl quality. I had no doubt in my mind we were good enough to go the distance—not after the journey of this season; not after watching our team grow bolder, better, more sure of itself quarter by quarter.

I knew how much sweat the players had expended in training.

I knew how much planning the coaches had done in preparation.

I knew how much devotion the city had expressed, spurring us on. This was the state of Tennessee's first taste of big-time NFL success. They were rabid, frenzied, and now silenced.

I knew the toll that talk-show second-guessing, sports page hindsight, and armchair quarterbacking had taken on my wife and kids.

Yet this had been our year. Up to this moment, at the sixteen-second mark, the whole season had unfolded like a fairy tale, too good to be true.

Maybe it *had* been too good to be true.

I looked down at the field, and suddenly I felt finished with the whole thing. Heartbreaking losses weren't anything new—I had been through the whole gamut of game-day emotions over the years. But somehow, this time it just seemed like too much. I was tired. This game of football, the vocation I'd been dedicated to for so many years, didn't seem to have an ounce of joy left in it. I heard myself whisper, "Lord, I never want to coach again."

I was shocked by my own thoughts, but I knew they were sincere. I felt terrible for the players; for the coaches; for our Head Coach Jeff Fisher; for our general manager; for our owner; for everyone in the state of Tennessee who desperately wanted to play in a Super Bowl.

Welcome to the Playoffs

Making the playoffs had been huge for the Titans. We had pointed to this opportunity. I can remember how it felt to step into the locker room during the countdown to kickoff. An NFL locker room is a fun place—guys joking, talking about their assignments, listening to music, putting on the pads. But on this day, you could taste the tension in the air. The room was full of raw nerves. We, the coaches, didn't need to say a word about what today meant. There was no need to light a fire under anyone. Everybody on the team, right down to the trainers, knew what was at stake.

We'd talked about it from the beginning of training camp three seasons ago, and here we were. Time to get it done on the field.

What a young group of guys this was. Only a handful of them had played in an NFL postseason game. I knew what these men were about to experience. I'd been in playoff games with other teams, even a Super Bowl. I knew how the adrenaline flowed in this kind of situation. I'd seen the difference in intensity between a Super Bowl game and a regular season game.

My own initiation to the postseason had come way back in 1980. I'd stood on the sidelines next to Bud Grant, legendary coach of the Minnesota Vikings, and it took about three or four plays into the game for me to notice the difference. These guys were playing as if their very lives depended on it. The pads weren't popping; they were *crashing.* The grunts and the cries of pain were louder and more frequent. Players were running hard, hitting hard, selling out on every play. This was nothing like the level of focus I had seen in the regular season. I remember turning to a hardened old-school veteran named Wally Hilgenberg and expressing my amazement. "What is this?" I asked. "Where did this crazy intensity come from?"

Hilgenberg had a good laugh when he saw my wide eyes. He said, "Welcome to the NFL playoffs, Coach."

Since then, I've been around the block a few times. Now I was the old-school guy, and I was the one welcoming these young men to the NFL playoffs. I saw more nervousness than intensity for the time being. But I knew the feeling was going to change as soon as these players stepped onto the field. In the meantime, I wasn't going to let all this nervousness change our game plan, our team identity, or all the preparation we'd done for this game. I knew what we were capable of doing. These were highly talented, competitive athletes who would rise to the challenge. Once they hit the turf, once they began to experience that fierce playoff atmosphere, they were going to be okay.

Yet the nerves carried over to the team introductions, those moments when the announcer calls out a name and that player sprints out to his moment in the spotlight. There are high fives, excited voices, a bit of showboating. It's all about fun.

But not today. As the Titans heard their names, they simply ran out and stood together on the field. They were not animated. They showed none of their characteristic exuberance. They were *solemn,* and solemn isn't a football thing.

I was thankful that the Buffalo Bills seemed just as tight. As the game began, both offenses played a bit tentatively. I looked mostly to our running back Eddie George and the ground game, hoping we could pound the Bills up the middle and wear them down in the second half. I knew we could count on our terrific defense, and sure enough, the Titans' "D" dominated the first two quarters. Buffalo managed only 64 yards, and just as important, they committed nine penalties.

But the first quarter ended scoreless. Two great defenses were dictating the pace. As a matter of fact, it was our defense that finally got us the first score. Three minutes into the second quarter, our linebacker, Jevon Kearse, broke around the right tackle and slammed into the Bills' quarterback, Rob Johnson, in the Buffalo end zone. The safety gave us a 2–0 lead. *Thanks, defense,* I thought. *Time for our side to do its share.* Maybe Kearse had given us the big play we needed to get untracked emotionally.

Geronimo!

My hopes were justified. On the free kick that follows every safety, we got another big play—this time from special teams. Our kick returner, Derrick Mason, found a seam in the coverage and sprinted forty-two yards down to the Buffalo 28. I knew we had to take advantage of this situation, especially the way Buffalo was playing on defense. I called the plays and thought, *Come on, men. Let's get it done.* We drove it down to the 2-yard line. Everybody knows how tough those last two yards are; the middle is jammed with linemen. The linebackers come up and fill in every gap. The defensive backs have only ten yards of end zone to cover.

I pulled out a play that has always been one of my favorites. We call it Geronimo, and it's actually a two-play combination that is designed to beat the goal-line defense and steal that final, longest yard. We signaled in the plays. Steve McNair, our quarterback, stepped into the huddle and said, "Listen up. Alert Geronimo, alert Geronimo, thirteen iso."

We'd practiced it over and over, and everybody knew what to do. On the immediate play, we would send our running back Eddie George right up the middle (the I-back in the 3-hole, in X and O terms). That was a simple power play, with "iso" meaning "isolation," a man-to-man, one-on-one blocking scheme with the fullback leading the running back up the middle. If Eddie didn't score, we hoped to take the defense by surprise. Then, as the tacklers were getting up from the turf, our players would sprint to the line without huddling, and Geronimo would be in effect.

Geronimo means "It's on GO," from the first and last letters. It's straight to the line with no huddle, and the quarterback quickly calls out, "Set-GO!" as the surprised defense tries to scramble into position. Steve fakes a handoff to Eddie George. George and the fullback vault over the line to draw the linebackers forward. Then Steve bootlegs to the outside with the option to run or pass to the tight end—whichever is open.

That's how it all played out in this case. We ran the first play, and the Bills stopped Eddie after a 1-yard gain. Geronimo then worked to perfection. Steve took the snap, rolled out, and saw that the defense chose to pick up the tight end. That left him free to practically skip into the end zone untouched.

Suddenly, after all the nerves and tightness, and all the frustration of the first quarter, we had a 9–0 lead and everyone had contributed: a defensive score, a special teams play, and a gimmick on the goal line. We'll take 'em however we get 'em.

From there, we had two more stalled drives. But just before half-time, we stole another one—though we did put a nice drive together this time: eleven plays, fifty-six yards. We passed, we ran, and it seemed as if the logjam was loosening up. Suddenly we were at the Buffalo 27. That's where the drive stalled. I thought, *If only we could get those last five yards, to the 22.* I call that yard line the "Magic 22," because it makes a 40-yard field goal possible. History teaches us that in the NFL, a kicker is almost always going to be accurate from that distance. Anything farther carries greater risk. I always told our players, "Get us the seven points. But failing that, at least make it to the Magic 22 so we can take something with us from the drive."

As it happened, our kicker, Al DelGreco, missed the 45-yard attempt from the 27. But once again, we got the break. Buffalo committed a 5-yard penalty on the play, and Al got a second shot—this time from the "magic" yard line. The kick sailed through, and we ran into the locker room very pleased with a 12–0 lead. Even so, I felt the defense was doing its job and we needed to pull our share of the load. In the second half I wanted to see us put some points on the board and put Buffalo away.

Do You Have Faith?

Yet it was Buffalo who came into the third quarter with new momentum. Antowain Smith broke loose on the first play and ran 44 yards before we could catch him. It was not an auspicious beginning to the half. The Bills drove a total of sixty-two yards to a touchdown by Smith. What a huge difference between a twelve-point lead and a five-point lead. Now we were concerned. As great as our defense was, it couldn't hold the line forever. I was frustrated because the offense had four possessions and came away with zero points. When you're the offensive coordinator in a big game, and it's the offense that is struggling, you feel responsible for the lack of production.

Then the fourth quarter began exactly like the third: Buffalo moving sixty-plus yards for an Antowain Smith touchdown. The score was 13–12, Buffalo's favor. They chose to attempt a two-point conversion to give themselves a field goal advantage, but the pass fell incomplete.

Just when it seemed we could lose a heartbreaker, we managed to put something together. We got a great punt return by Isaac Byrd, then Eddie George began to fight his way to some tough yards. That playoff intensity was definitely there. Both sides were selling out on every play, pounding each other as if there were no tomorrow—which is true in the postseason.

We got Al DelGreco set up inside the Magic 22 for a 36-yard field goal. We had the lead back with only 1:48 remaining in the game.

After a score, there is always an element of relief. You can almost feel a sigh in the press box and on the sidelines. *We did it! Come on, defense.* And it's great to know you have that dominating D that can become a brick wall when everything is on the line. Coordinator Gregg Williams' men knew how to finish strong. But defenses get tired after three and a half quarters too. As I watched the Bills work themselves down the field with their two-minute offense, I felt the game slipping away. I wondered if there was something more we could have done on offense—some way to have earned seven points and put the game on ice. I had elected to take the field goal because that's the percentage play. A field goal is less of a gamble on third and long. We had Al DelGreco, and the kick was going to give us the winning margin. Then he'd made it. So I knew I'd made the right decision.

Still—it was devastating to sit and watch Buffalo rolling down the field. They hit two passes followed by a 12-yard run, and all of a sudden they were in position to kick a field goal to win the game. Buffalo brought in Steve Christie for a 41-yard field goal attempt. Only twenty seconds remained on the clock, so this had to be for the game, for survival in the postseason. We called our first timeout to "ice" the kicker—the only weapon we had left in our arsenal.

Those waits seemed to last forever. I had time to ask myself where our lead had gone. How had this one gotten away from us? I had time to think that maybe Christie would miss—hey, forty-one yards is not automatic. I watched the kicker trot onto the field; I saw the snap, the hold, the kick, and the ball sailed through the uprights.

Bills on top. Sixteen seconds left to oblivion.

That's when my spirits finally reached bottom. Coaching had been the only career I had known, but this was too much. There had been something particularly critical about this game for our young team. Nashville wanted it so badly. The players and coaches wanted it. And now, to have led most of the game and to fall short by one point . . .

"Lord, I never want to coach again," I had prayed moments earlier. "I've had it."

Then I had one of those extraordinary moments: I heard the quiet voice of God.

I heard him ask, *Do you have faith?*

I know what you're thinking. But listen, this isn't something that happens to me on an everyday basis. I can tell you that when it does, the words, the message, and the source are unmistakable. I answered the question immediately and instinctively.

"Yes, Lord, I have faith."

And just like that, I had hope. I can't explain it even today, but I was excited even as everyone around me had given up. Sure, I was tense. But I was hopeful that something good was going to happen.

Do You Believe in Miracles?

Steve Walters, who coached our receivers, was sitting beside me. He heard my words, saw my face, and probably thought I had lost my mind. I wouldn't have blamed him. But at the moment, I didn't really care. I was too busy watching the field to see what came next.

Chris, my wife, sat in the section reserved for team families. Her heart sank with those around her. She saw how everyone there had given up. By her side was our son Christian, disbelief written across his face. Nearby, Tom Rogeberg, a close friend, offered the only hint of hope from the next seat: "Remember, all things are possible . . ."

Chris nodded—she knew the verse—but her faith was running low. She couldn't know that at this very second, my own faith had kicked into high gear.

Alan Lowry, our special teams coach, sent in a special play. We had practiced it over and over but had never tried it in a game. It was the kind of play you save for a rainy day, and that rainy day had certainly come.

Lowry's play called for a lateral from whoever received the kick. He would turn around and toss the ball to our tight end, Frank Wycheck. Then Wycheck would make a second lateral—this time to Kevin Dyson, across the field, who had the wheels to speed into the end zone. The double pitch would hopefully turn the Bills' coverage inside out, and Dyson could turn on the burners and streak down the far sideline.

Well, you know how these desperation plays are—they look great on paper. Realistically, we were looking at a long shot. Among other things, no matter how often you practice the play, a live game situation will throw some completely unexpected variable at you.

That's exactly what happened. Our fullback, Lorenzo Neal, ran up and caught the kickoff; that was a miracle in itself, because Lorenzo wasn't known for his great hands.

Throw it to Wycheck, Lorenzo! But for some reason, Neal *ran* to our tight end and personally delivered the ball.

Who'd have figured it? The improvised handoff could have blown up the play, but it did the opposite. As the Bills rapidly converged on Wycheck, at the last possible second he lofted a perfect spiral to Kevin Dyson, who was standing wide open. Kevin caught it on his back foot and saw what seemed to be a thousand acres of empty real estate in front of him. Dyson locked the ball away and galloped seventy-five yards down the field untouched, scoring the six most breathtaking points I had ever witnessed.

The stadium gave way to instant pandemonium. Our players came off the bench and sprinted to the end zone to celebrate, creating a pileup on Kevin Dyson that made us wonder if he was going to emerge. The Titans' radio announcer said, "This is insanity!"

"Miracle!" the TV commentators screamed as they ran the instant replay over and over. Some sportswriter was busy coining the phrase *Music City Miracle.* That handle would stick, and the play would abide in NFL lore along with Franco Harris's Immaculate Reception of 1972 and Drew Pearson's Hail Mary catch of 1975. New as we were to the league, we had our moment in history to ensure that everyone would remember the Titans.

Roll the Tape

But it wasn't over yet. As we expected, the wild play was under review by the officials. The Bills were contending that the throw to Dyson had been not a lateral but a forward pass, which would be illegal on a kickoff. If the ball travels even a freckle forward, it's not a lateral but a forward pass. There was no doubt that it was indeed a very close call.

If the Bills won their argument, then our miracle would be one more bubble that burst, and the pain of falling short would cut even deeper. The ref peered into the little instant replay monitor as time stood still. But I believed! After all, true miracles are seldom over-ruled by zebras.

Up in the press box, we felt that two little factors weighed in our favor. First, ESPN's Joe Theismann diagrammed the play onscreen with the TV marker. He quickly scrawled a line representing the throw, and his mark happened to slant in a clearly lateral direction (though the true arc of the ball was more vertical). That little squig-gle helped our case with the viewers at home. Second, the head line judge had initially signaled a lateral the moment Dyson caught the ball. There had to be "clear evidence" of a forward pass to overrule the official's on-the-spot call. I felt my body relaxing.

The head of the officiating crew finally trotted forward and said, "After further review, the play stands." His hands shot toward heaven, and he said, "Touchdown." The fan celebration began all over again, even wilder than the first time.

That's what I call putting an exclamation point on a remarkable season. From the press box where I sat, I saw coaches and fans danc-ing together like children on Christmas morning. It was a moment to cherish forever.

I was unlikely to forget the incredible play; the pass that somehow became a handoff—and of course, Dyson's sprint to glory. But most of all, I would carry with me the memory of that powerful lesson: *God is in control. Therefore, no matter what situation arises in life, we never lose hope.* Surprises may lie just around the corner.

As I sat and savored the feeling of victory, a favorite verse came to mind—Proverbs 21:31 in the *Living Bible* paraphrase: "Go ahead and prepare for the conflict, but victory comes from God." *Make your game plan as if it's all on you; go into the battle as if it's all on God.* I've often reminded myself that no matter how well I plan, I can't control the movements of twenty-two players (offensive and defensive) on the field when the ball is snapped. But I know the one who can.

I've seen those diagrams of hurricanes that tear through the countryside with incredibly destructive power yet with perfect calm at the center point—the eye of the storm. I had come to a place in my life where I had finally learned how to rest within that spiritual center of peace instead of being at the mercy of my career and its turbulent winds.

I think that's why God asked me, "Do you have faith?" The question is whether I really believe he is in control of everything, good and bad—all of it. Can I trust him when I reach the peak of success? Can I trust him when I crash on the rocks?

Who's in Control Here?

This book tells the story of how a driven life finally found its resting place; how a restless marine finally stilled the battle in his own soul.

I guess I had been hearing the question all my life:

Do you have faith?

Sure, Lord, but I just need one more promotion.

Do you have faith?

Of course I do, Lord, but I think I need to work harder, do more.

Do you have faith?

Absolutely. But, God, can't you give me what I want first?

I finally understood that he wasn't looking for the long answer. He wanted to hear it short and simple, as from a child: *Yes, Lord, I have faith.*

This is also a story about how difficult it can be to finally learn that lesson, yet how powerfully God comes through when we place our trust in him.

I want to tell you about a little kid on a school bus in seventh grade, tears of frustration on his face because he isn't allowed to play the sport he loves; about the anger that begins to grow within that child.

I want to tell you about that same boy in high school, standing in the kitchen in full football pads, begging his dad to sign the permission slip allowing him to play, just an hour before the season opener.

There's that young man who practices for four years on a college football team, taking physical punishment as a walk-on without ever dressing out or playing in a real game, and who later proclaims that the last thing in the world he will ever be is a football coach.

Finally, there is a story of marine buddies and one young woman who believed in the boy-turned-man and encouraged him to explore that unlikely career anyway.

Most of all, I want to tell you how it could be that such a person, who played in a handful of high school football games and none in college, somehow became one of the youngest men to ascend to the position of head coach in the National Football League—only to suffer bitter defeat and humiliation.

I'd also like to say a word or two about a crowning moment; how a man can coach in two Super Bowls yet find the deepest and most rewarding experience of his career afterward, with an amazing group of teenagers on a high school gridiron.

In all these highs and lows, through every moment of this unlikely chain of events, there is only one constant: the truth that God really does have a plan, and his plan is better and wiser and more fulfilling than any strategy a coach could diagram on a chalkboard.

I've heard it said that we learn the greatest lessons through adversity. If that's true, I ought to be a genius by now. I don't know any football coach who has been fired as many times as I have. I expect to be the first inductee in the Pink Slip Hall of Fame, if they ever build one. Yet I can honestly tell you that I hold no bitterness about any of it. As life moves along, I have an increasing gratitude for the path my life has taken—for the pits as well as the peaks—because I think I have some idea of what my Creator has been up to. I can see now that whatever career goals I may have missed along the way, they were more than worth exchanging for the joy of attaining the ones God had for me.

I definitely felt gratitude during one of those peaks, when I sat in the press box on the eighth day of year 2000 and savored a team victory in the Music City Miracle. I realized that God was in control, I wasn't, and therefore I had permission to hope.

Do I believe God reached down from heaven and lifted Kevin Dyson into the end zone during an AFC wild card playoff game? No, of course not.

Do I believe God even cares what happens in a football game?

Absolutely!

I know there are those who believe the outcome of a sporting event is too trivial for divine attention. The Lord has the fate of nations to worry about, they say. He has earthquakes and wars and crises on every front, so wouldn't the petty events inside a football stadium land several hundred notches down his priority list?

On top of that, what about those good folks on the other sideline? God loves *both* teams, right?

Of course he does. But the heavenly Father I know and love is one who cares about everything that happens—yes, even in football games.

The Extra Point

Let me put the question right back to you:

Do you think the Lord of the universe cares about your day at the office?

Do you think God is paying attention to that housewife vacuuming behind the sofa, or the little girl playing on the swing set?

What are the big concerns in your life right now? I suggest you stop and make a list. Are you worried about your job? Your health? Your family? Any problems at home?

The biggest question of all is this: What makes you think any of that is too trivial for a perfect, loving God who created us to be his children? I believe he is right there with us in the dust of the details, because he is the Lord of all of it. He cares deeply about whatever we care deeply about, because he loves us with an everlasting love. My wife, Chris, and I talk to our three kids on our cell phones almost constantly, and I can tell you we're interested in what they have for lunch, what books they're reading, and how they are feeling about life in general. There is no "trivial." What matters to our children matters to us.

Parents are like that. And that's what God is, after all—the most loving and attentive parent there could be. He is a dad, not a chairman of the board. I believe he is great enough that there are no little things with him, nor any little people.

Let's go back to that list you made a minute ago—the list of stuff that's on your mind right now. Your worries, your hopes, your dreams. It's like emptying your mental wallet to see what has collected in there. I challenge you to think again about every one of those items and realize that God cares about it as much as you do.

- That big project at work—it's on God's daily planner too. He wants you to do your best.
- Your marriage—God is the one who put it together. He wants it to bring you joy.
- Your children—they're his children too.
- You might as well add your golf game, the car you're interested in buying, the vacation that's in the planning stages. You can't name

a single issue that isn't a God issue, simply for the reason that he cares very much about you.

Step into tomorrow with that thought firmly in mind. Your miracle may be right around the corner.

2

One Yard Short

GUN SPEAR Right OPEN ZAG FIRM SLIVER - DETROIT

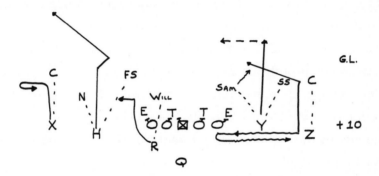

In the rich annals of NFL history, there are a select few truly classic plays. I'm certain that no team other than the 1999 Tennessee Titans has experienced *two* of them in one postseason. Actually, I doubt it has ever happened in baseball, basketball, hockey, soccer, or professional tiddledywinks. But in the first days of a new century, it happened to us. There was the double-lateral against the Bills, and then, in the Super Bowl . . .

But let's not get ahead of ourselves.

To appreciate the full impact of that wild postseason, you really have to know something about the Titan family's journey. What a ride we'd had.

You might remember that our franchise had been known for many years as the Houston Oilers—a team that never appeared in a Super Bowl. The franchise moved to Tennessee before the state was quite ready for us. That is, we had no home stadium. We had to play for a year in Memphis while living and practicing in Nashville. We were a team without a city or a permanent name, because we were still the Tennessee *Oilers* at that point.

This was an odd situation for an NFL team, being a team without a town; an orphan franchise. It's easy to understand why the city of Memphis was less than galvanized by the idea of hosting a "layover" team. Remember, Memphis had wanted a franchise of its own but had lost out to Nashville. The two cities have always been rivals, and Memphis didn't easily embrace this temporary "home team." Transition took its toll. During our year of displacement, we could do no better than an indifferent 8–8 record.

The next year, 1998, we arrived in Nashville. But the new Adelphia Coliseum remained under construction. Consequently, we played our games in the cozier confines that are the home of Vanderbilt University's football team.

Tennessee had long been college football country, and the Southeastern Conference ruled people's affections. And it so happened that the University of Tennessee Volunteers were in the process of winning a national championship in 1998. Maybe that's one reason the Nashville fans were a little tentative in accepting us. We played before some tiny crowds—quite strange in the NFL, where many cities pack the house. And we picked up where we left off, losing three of our first four games. Yet you could see that something special was just around the corner. Our dynamic Head Coach Jeff Fisher was moving us forward with strong leadership in a challenging time.

We had young men like Steve McNair and Eddie George, to mention two, who were raising the level of their game every week. Our general manager, Floyd Reese, had filled the stable with thoroughbreds. We rallied and began to win in November and December but just missed the playoffs with another 8–8 season.

Our fans definitely wanted their own NFL stadium. As Shoeless Joe said, "Build it and they will come." The fans also wanted their own name. "Oilers" didn't make sense, because we weren't in Texas anymore. So the Houston Oilers became the Tennessee Oilers became the Tennessee Titans. New name, new home, new uniforms, a new day. Training camp and the 1999 season were about to begin.

Then, on the morning of July 8, we opened the Nashville newspaper and spotted the following headline: "Playoffs or Pink Slips."

The team owner was speaking out in a candid interview. It was time for make-or-break, in his judgment. He said he knew that the head coach and general manager understood that their jobs depended on a playoff berth. "I don't really need to tell them; I think they understand where we are coming from," he said in the article. He pointed out that three straight years of 8–8 football was not going to be acceptable, not with the roster's talent level. The owner expressed optimism that we would indeed take our game to championship level.

But the message couldn't have been clearer. *Playoff or be run off.* The coaching staff came into the season with a greater-than-usual sense of urgency.

A Wild Ride to Atlanta

The owner's ultimatum was just the beginning of the ride. We coaches braced for battle, updated the playbooks—and just like that, lost our quarterback. Steve McNair had a serious back injury. According to the surgeon, McNair would sit out the entire season. As the offensive coordinator, I had built all my plans around Steve and his special gifts. The season hadn't even begun, and already it felt less like the Titans and more like the *Titanic*—a sinking ship. It was easy to conclude that our offensive fortunes were as damaged as Steve's back. Was I going to have to move my family one more time?

I remember talking it over with Chris, my wife. "Who knows what lies ahead?" we said. "Let's just pray that God receives the glory and wait to see what he has in store for us."

What God had in store was a special team, a special season, and ultimately a special calling.

The season began with a flourish. We could have lost our first game in Adelphia—an offensive shootout. We hung tough and won it 36–35 on an Al DelGreco field goal with only seconds remaining. After that, there was some kind of bond between our team and its stadium. We had a perfect record on the home field.

I think about so many memorable games of that season. For example, who could forget the first of three epic battles with Jacksonville that year? It was played in the midst of a torrential rainstorm on the road. Up in the press box, I called plays through a window that was like a windshield with no wipers. There were times when it was all I could do to see the field. And down on that messy turf, we depended on our backup quarterback, Neil O'Donnell. He came through for us in a big way.

Neil brought know-how and leadership to a young team. He had been to a Super Bowl already, and he could tell the guys what that experience was like and what it would require of them. I admired Neil for his dedication physically and mentally in learning the game plans each week. He would come in every Wednesday and get the game plan, with all its checks and audibles. This was his first year in our system, so initially he would struggle with the details. "Why are we doing this?" he would ask. "And why this one over here?" I would just laugh and tell him to stop driving me crazy. Then Neil would go home, come back the next morning, and announce that he had the whole thing mastered.

It says a lot for the Titans and for Neil in particular that we had to take the field without our starting quarterback for five games and still made it to Atlanta. Neil's leadership held it all together on offense as we won four during a critical five-game stretch. He absolutely refused to force a pass and create a turnover. Avoidance of turnovers is one of the hallmarks of my offensive philosophy, so I appreciated him.

Neil wasn't the only player to step up. That first Jacksonville game ended on a dramatic note, as the Jaguars threw the ball into the end zone instead of settling for a tying field goal. Samari Rolle, our young cornerback, picked off the pass and sealed the victory for us.

Meanwhile, Steve McNair devoted himself to rehabilitation and made it back after only five weeks. Remember, we had been told he was gone for the year. His quick return was a medical miracle in itself. As the season progressed, we began to get it going on offense, defense, and special teams. The Titans cruised through the regular season at 13–3 (9–1 in our division, where it counted most). Steve McNair was brilliant once he made it back, and Eddie George was a rugged and aggressive running back. On the other side of the ball, Jevon Kearse was making his impact as Defensive Rookie of the Year. We were playing as a team as never before.

Road Warriors

Even so, we had to enter the postseason through the back door. At 13–3, we actually had the second best record in our division, so we had to be satisfied with a wild card slot. That's how we found ourselves playing Buffalo in that unforgettable playoff of January 8, 2000, as detailed in the first chapter.

It's easy to forget that even with the Music City Miracle, a long road lay ahead to Super Bowl XXXIV. A wild card team receives no bye week—it must play a first round game immediately. That's a significant disadvantage, because you're fighting for your life while the next opponent is resting and preparing. Also, we knew we had to spend our postseason in unfriendly environs. At Adelphia we'd been perfect; now it was all about getting it done on the road.

Our divisional playoff was in Indianapolis, where we faced Peyton Manning and the favored Colts. As the players and coaches stepped onto the turf for pregame stretching and warm-ups, I listened to the encouraging sound of cheering. Even with an away game, several thousand faithful Titan fans had come up the highway with us and bought their tickets from scalpers. That's dedication. NFL teams really appreciate the "Road Warrior" fans who follow us across America, making us feel home away from home. We had a strong home-team presence in every city we visited, but never as strong as that day in the RCA Dome.

As we prepared to kick off against the Colts, I found Jim Mora, their head coach, a longtime friend. Jim and his wife, Connie, were there when Chris and I were married. He was a marine officer like me, and we had served together on the Colorado University staff when I was just breaking into this profession. That day Jim sized me up and said, "Hey, you look pretty relaxed, Les."

He was right. Our players were ready, and I was ready. I had looked into our men's eyes and had seen a different team than the one that had been so tentative, so anxious and solemn, before the wild card game one week earlier. They had gotten the playoff butterflies out of their stomachs. They were loose, relaxed, and beginning to believe. The expression I saw on their faces said, *We can do this.* Coaches have seen this phenomenon: a play like the Music City Miracle provides a "team of destiny" feel. Athletes start to have the idea they are meant to win, meant to go the distance. Opponents hate running into that level of confidence.

The Indianapolis game was an odd one, a kicker's game, really. We had four field goals, the Colts had three, and each team scored one touchdown. But just as important as Al DelGreco's kicks was the running of Eddie George behind the offensive line led by future Hall of Famer Bruce Matthews. Eddie ran an awesome 162 yards for the day, including one run of sixty-eight on the third play of the third quarter.

His big run had to be the play of the game. We called it 17 Switch, but what made it special was that our right tackle, Jon Runyan, improvised on the play. In other words, he pulled to the left rather than running it the way we actually had it drawn up for him. Sometimes it just works out better when you don't do things perfectly. With Runyan to the left side, we had an extra blocker at the point of attack, creating a hole you could have driven a Hummer limousine through. It looked as though he could have invited several other running backs to go with him. Eddie broke to the right side, headed for the massive opening, and thundered toward our only touchdown of the day.

I'll also never forget our punt to Indianapolis later in the third quarter. Their punt returner caught the ball on the 10 and returned it eighty-seven yards to our 3. That play would have been disastrous for us. But Al DelGreco, who was having a busy enough day as it was, ran up to Jeff Fisher, shouting, "He stepped out of bounds! He stepped out of bounds!" Could it be true? We called for a review of the play, and Al turned out to be just as accurate with his eyes as he was with his foot. The replay showed that the returner had touched the sideline chalk at the Colts' 34.

What a game saver! When a special season is finally over, and you make it to the Super Bowl, it's easy to forget these turning-point moments that allowed you to keep going. I hate to be the ten thousandth person to observe that football is a game of inches, but the reason they keep saying it is that it's so true.

In the end, with our fans voicing their devotion, we finished off the Colts by a score of 19–16 and punched our ticket to the next round.

Champions

So far, so good. We had notched one wild card miracle and one second round victory, and now we faced an even bigger challenge. That's the way the postseason goes, with the stakes climbing every week.

This time the site was Jacksonville for the AFC Championship game. The winner would be bound for Atlanta and a spot in the Super Bowl. The Jaguars had finished ahead of us at 14–2 in our division—with both of their losses to us. But we could not be overconfident. In our league it's asking a great deal to beat any team three times in a season, particularly a fourteen-win powerhouse like Jacksonville. In fact, it had never been done.

That "third time is the charm" angle may explain why Jacksonville was so confident. The city was planning victory parades. The stadium was circled by cars with big Super Bowl XXXIV stickers on them. They expected to be there, because surely no one could beat them three times in one season—when no else in the league had beaten them at all. Atlanta isn't too far from Jacksonville, and the Jaguar fans were ready to make that trip.

The Jaguars got off to a good start. Midway through the third quarter, we were behind 14–10. But the Titans hung tough. We proceeded to score twenty-three unanswered points and put the game away. Finally, here was the offensive explosion we had been waiting for, and I enjoyed every moment of it. Steve McNair, who had spent much of the week wearing a special boot to protect an injured toe, scrambled all over the field and ran for two scores. He also threw a touchdown pass to Yancey Thigpen, who left the game with a broken toe himself. Even in the midst of such a big victory, the loss of Thigpen was a crushing blow to our postseason hopes.

We scored sixteen points in four and a half minutes. Sometimes it happens like that—a game just suddenly turns and one side takes total control. A squeaker becomes a rout. Our defense forced six turnovers, the offense scored repeatedly, and the Jaguar fans sat in total shock. Remember, this team had the best record in the league. No one but the Titans had beaten them, and now it was happening for the third time: the hat trick.

While the game was still close, we sacked Mark Brunell in the end zone for a safety. Then, on the ensuing free kick, Derrick Mason took the ball eighty yards for a touchdown. That was the crushing blow. Everyone in the stadium could feel it. After Derrick's return, we began to pour it on, cruising to a 33–14 victory that punched our ticket to Atlanta for Super Bowl XXXIV.

After the game a wild and jubilant team celebrated in a silent and sullen stadium. I hurried down the stairs to the field, where the rest of the Titans were gathering for the AFC Championship ceremony. Our owner Bud Adams, Head Coach Jeff Fisher, and captain Bruce Matthews hoisted the trophy over their heads as the faithful Titans fans, who once again had made the pilgrimage from Tennessee, roared their approval from the visitors' "cheap seats." Jaguar fans were swarming the exits. As for me, I didn't head for the platform. I've always looked first for my family, so I was scanning the Titans' section for them. Suddenly our oldest son Christian appeared on the front row. Just like that, he climbed onto the retaining wall and leaped to the field to give me a big hug. But just as suddenly he was gone—grabbed by security guards and hustled away toward the tunnel.

"Hey!" I yelled. "That's my son!"

"Fans can't come on the field," growled a Jacksonville guard.

Christian somehow maneuvered his way back into the stadium and into the celebrating locker room where I had made my way. "Nice security, huh?" he said with a grin.

There's nothing in the world like the feeling in a locker room after you win a championship game. It's just total, raucous, wall-to-wall joy. You've worked so hard for so long, and now you've earned a trophy that no one can take away. Anticipation gives way to celebration.

In the midst of all the laughter and shouting, there was a quiet moment I'll always cherish. Jackie Harris, an outstanding tight end, grabbed me with one big, sweaty forearm and whispered, "Coach, the reason why we're here is that you've been faithful." With all the other emotions we were already feeling, his words put me over the edge. I'll never forget that.

The Super Bowl was waiting for us. We tried to let that mind-blowing fact sink in. Could it really be true? Only months before, we had faced the possibility of losing our jobs if we failed to make the playoffs. Now we had done more than survive that ultimatum. We were going for the big prize—a world championship trophy.

Tired but Triumphant

When we flew home, the grateful city of Nashville was waiting en masse at the airport. We had no idea there would be such a reception. It took about an hour and a half for us to make it through thousands of screaming, adoring fans. I'd never experienced anything like it. Everybody associated with the team was mobbed. For so long the Titans hadn't had a home; it certainly appeared that we had one now. This was a far cry from the quiet confines of the Liberty Bowl in Memphis.

Everyone loaded into the waiting buses, and police escorts led us to the stadium for an even larger celebration. We loved partying with our fans, but we were dog-tired after three emotional, physical weeks of facing the best NFL competition. Here we were preparing for the Super Bowl as a wild card team without something we crucially needed: a week off.

Football fans know that when the NFC and AFC playoffs are completed, usually there is an open week before the Super Bowl. Therefore, the two teams have fourteen days to rest and get ready for the final battle. The media has two weeks to do its thing with hype and publicity.

But this wasn't the case in January 2000. That year the Super Bowl came immediately on the following weekend. As a wild card team, we had to play through without a week off. It seemed as if we hadn't rested in forever. A lot of players were injured or banged up, and we were a staff of mentally exhausted coaches who needed more time to build a game plan.

For any team, NFL coaching means working from 5:30 a.m. until 10:00 p.m. or later during the season. Then it's time to rise and shine and strategize some more. This routine simply goes with the territory from July through January. If you're fortunate enough to make it all the way to the Super Bowl, your schedule grows even more rugged. Now you feel the accumulation of pushing yourself for so many months; of preparing for nineteen games plus four exhibition games on the other end. And now, just as there's not too much of you left, you have to reach down for something extra, because this is the biggest game of your life. This is the Super Bowl. So now you're working and planning until two or three in the morning and still rising at five thirty.

In addition to this challenge, you're immersed in a wild atmosphere all through the week leading up to the big game. Player's and coaches' families are deciding who uses the tickets. Press calls are coming in not just from the local newspapers but from all over the world. There are media sessions and bright television lights every day. The Super Bowl is the most watched television event on the face of the earth. It's a global media event.

So there's all this extra craziness topping off the usual NFL coaching craziness. You can hardly stop to take a breath, to think, to savor the moment, or to get your spiritual bearings. As the offensive coordinator, I carried an even greater load.

I think back on that week in Atlanta, and I remember a whirlwind:

Both sets of our parents flying in.

Watching hours and hours of game film on our opponent, the St. Louis Rams.

Climbing out of bed one more time after three hours of sleep.

Practicing with the team on the campus of Georgia Tech near downtown Atlanta.

Talking to the men; keeping them focused.

Riding around town in an RV with Al Michaels and Boomer Esiason, talking Xs and Os for an ABC-TV feature.

Jogging in a rare Atlanta ice storm.

Welcoming Dr. Charles Stanley to speak at our chapel service.

Of course, all of it becomes insane when two weeks of media overkill are squeezed into one. There wasn't time to sleep. There wasn't even time to think. Suddenly there we were in the Georgia Dome with the crowd roaring and the cameras running; the lineup introductions, the national anthem, the coin toss, and finally, an actual, no-nonsense game of football.

XXXIV

It's quite an experience to walk onto a field that you know has the eyes of the world on it.

Don't believe anyone who tries to tell you it's just another day, just another game. If you don't have a churning stomach, if you don't feel the electricity in the air, if every nerve in your body isn't alive—well, maybe you just don't understand what makes this game so special and why all those millions of people across the world are watching in the first place.

I had been in big games—college bowl games, playoffs—but this one was for the world championship of football. As I came out onto the gridiron, the air was alive with anticipation. There are a select few sporting events in America that have that amazing vibrancy that infects the crowd and makes the air so electric that the spine tingles. The opening of the gates at the Kentucky Derby, for instance, is one of those moments. Anyone who has been there knows what I mean. The noise rises to pandemonium level and just hangs there forever. You could sense it at Yankee Stadium in the seventh game of the World Series, or when the announcer says, "Gentleman, start your engines," at the Indy 500.

As kickoff drew closer for Super Bowl XXXIV, we watched our players move through the usual pregame stretching and warm-ups. The usual coaches' chatter was absent. Everyone stood almost reverently, awed by the atmosphere. I know each of us was trying to take hold of a moment that comes perhaps once in life and savor it even as we prepared for battle. I had passed this way once before in Super Bowl XX, but fourteen years had come and gone in my life. I had raised a family, traveled my own emotional journey, and hopefully matured as a coach and as a man. I felt that same electricity that infected everyone else. Still, I wanted to display calm and composure for my players. I had always admired leaders such as Tom Landry, who stood firm under fire, and I wanted to give our offense the same leadership.

S*tay focused, Les,* I told myself. *Stay in that mental tunnel and don't come out.* I refused to let the hype distract me from the job ahead of us. The pregame workout seemed to drag on forever. I was eager to get it out of the way, find my place upstairs, and get to work. I'm sure the staff of the St. Louis Rams was feeling the same thing. *Let's get into our seats and start this great chess match—winner take all.*

Stepping into the locker room, I looked from face to face and realized how special this group of men was. Every team is a unique unit that will never be assembled again. Free agency, the draft, retirement, injuries—all these variables ensure that next year's team will be different from this year's. And when you come to your final game together, your final locker room talk, your final battle, you feel a bittersweet awareness that this is the last go-around for a one-of-a-kind group of men.

I looked at Frank Wycheck and realized I was seeing the embodiment of the Titan personality—a blue-collar, hardworking player who was always going to make the big catch in the clutch; his dad was a Philadelphia cop. Frank had been cut by the Washington Redskins a few seasons back, but we picked him up, gave him a shot, and watched him grow to become the tight end who led the team in receptions during our big year.

My eyes moved along to Chris Sanders, a terrific wide receiver and an example of the explosive talent a championship team needs. A great deep threat, a track star from Ohio State, Chris was a playmaker. But he was also a wonderful human being. I had watched him kneel before his locker, preparing himself spiritually before a game.

Then, of course, Steve McNair—a young quarterback who hadn't played his first two seasons in the league but had waited his turn. He came out of Alcorn State University, and some had doubted he could lead an NFL team. Chris and I had attended his wedding one hot summer day in Vicksburg, Mississippi, and begun a rewarding friendship. Before our move to Nashville, he would come to our home during the off-season to talk about the mechanics of football. As Chris cooked us a meal, I would move saltshakers and artificial sweetener packets around the tabletop to simulate Xs and Os. Then we would move upstairs to watch hours of game film. He worked tirelessly mentally and physically to learn his craft, and his effort had gotten him all the way to the Super Bowl. Seeing young men get better—that's my hot button.

I looked at Eddie George and thought immediately of his rookie year. So many athletes never make it past their first sweaty August training camp. But here was Eddie George, Heisman trophy winner, moving through conditioning drills as if he were taking a Sunday walk through the park: 40-yard shuttle runs, 60-yard sprints. We would give the athletes a short rest, run them, rest them, run them, on and on. We called them suicide sprints. I can still see rows of athletes bent over with their hands on their knees, gasping for breath—all of them but one. There was Eddie George, standing tall, ready for his next sprint. I quickly spotted him for a thoroughbred and told myself, "We're going to run this guy. We're going to run him a lot." And I watched him take over games with his feet while rallying the team with his words. He was the vocal leader.

Bruce Matthews, on the other hand, let his actions do the talking. He was fierce as a competitor, quiet as a leader—though not too quiet off the field. Bruce was one of the most playful people I knew. Before practices, everyone gathered around him as he invented crazy games off the top of his head. He would grab some stray item such as a pylon and build a whole game around it. He would make up the rules and get everyone competing as if it counted. Then, at a crucial point in the season, he would stand up and have his say. "I just want to remind everybody—like they say, it's amazing what can be accomplished when no one cares who gets the credit." When he did speak out, everyone listened.

I looked at these men who meant so much to me, and I knew they were ready. *Stay in the tunnel, Les,* I thought again. *Don't look in the stands. Don't get caught up by the hype. Don't think about anything else. Just go do your job.*

Finally—the game. Super Bowls of the past have too often been blowouts. All that anticipation, all that expensive advertising time, and then more often than not the game itself is decided by halftime. I wasn't very happy to see Super Bowl XXXIV heading in that very direction as the first quarter got going. The Rams opened up a lead, but it could have been worse. Kurt Warner actually threw for a phenomenal 277 yards in the first half. The Rams outgained us 294–89, yet it was only 9–0 at the half. Three drives in a row (to the 12, to the 10, and to the 11) ended in field goals by Jeff Wilkins. Our defense became very tough around the goal line, and twenty-one potential points became nine when they stood firm.

But we didn't even have a field goal. *Oh please, not a goose egg!* I thought. Here we were with the whole world watching our offense. Nothing could be more humiliating than a shutout. But I knew that regardless of how big this game was, our players had pushed themselves to the limit. Many of them were playing with injuries. On defense, we came in without safety Marcus Robinson, and then, during the game, another safety, All-Pro Blaine Bishop, was knocked out with yet another injury. On the offensive side, we were really missing wide receiver Yancey Thigpen.

It bothered me that we were struggling in the ground game. We had thirty yards rushing at the half. During intermission we regrouped in the locker room. I remember challenging our offense. "Do you remember what we said?" I shouted. "We said we're gonna run the football, and we haven't done it. We're gonna get it done in the second half!" I remember grabbing Eddie George and Bruce Matthews, shaking them, and seeing the competitive fire that was still in their eyes. We just needed to believe. Forget 16–0. We were capable of exploding, and we just needed to light the fuse.

Jeff and the coaches knew we'd beaten these same Rams in the regular season. In October we had been on top at 21–0 by the end of the first quarter. It was the first game with McNair back from his surgery, and we'd whipped them. I knew we could beat these guys again. I reminded our men, "Zero turnovers guarantees victories." That was our hallmark during the season.

We came out and hung tough in the third quarter. But with just under four minutes left in that period, Warner finally hit a touchdown pass to Torry Holt. That made the score 16–0. Could we come up with three scores while shutting them out the rest of the game?

It was only two plays later that we lost Blaine Bishop with a neck sprain. The game stopped for ten minutes while Bishop was examined by doctors and finally carried from the field on a stretcher. Coaches and players on both sides forgot the game and prayed for Blaine during those minutes. The Titans could have given up at that point. It would be that much harder to hold off the Ram receivers with our two starting safeties out with injuries.

Yet something amazing happened. When the game resumed, our offense started to roll. Our guys suddenly seized control of a football game they'd been losing from the opening whistle. In the fourth quarter we held the ball for thirteen minutes. We ran thirty-two plays to only six for St. Louis—remarkable stats. We had a team that believed in itself, that wouldn't give up. You could see the confidence in the players' eyes as they slowly turned around a game that had been one-sided up to now.

Not only did we hold the ball, but we put it into the end zone, scoring two consecutive touchdowns by Eddie George. We went for two after the first touchdown, but the play failed.

The seconds were ticking away too quickly now. Just before the two-minute warning in the fourth quarter, we managed to drive to an Al DelGreco field goal that tied the score at 16–16. The stage was set for the greatest ending in Super Bowl history.

One Play, One Shot, One Yard

Now we were inside the two-minute mark. A packed house was on its feet, everybody screaming. Nobody was leaving the Georgia Dome early for postgame cocktail parties. Nobody in the TV audience, I trust, was switching channels. We were all tied up, and one of us was going to win, while the other was going to lose. The next one hundred and twenty seconds, played out by two exhausted squads of world-class athletes, would tell the story.

With renewed hope we kicked off after our tying field goal. And then a nightmare. On the first play of the series, the Rams' Kurt Warner threw downfield to Isaac Bruce. The ball was high, but Bruce made a terrific play on it, taking it away from our cornerback at the 38. Our defensive back fell down, and Bruce sprinted all the way into the end zone. I thought of our two injured safeties who might have made the stop. But it was a 73-yard touchdown, and the Rams were celebrating. We'd had them worried for the entire second half, and now they felt they had broken our spirits.

Could we fight back one more time? How many comebacks can you ask your guys to make? Not that you have to ask them—this is the Super Bowl. Every last Titan was willing to leave every ounce of sweat on the field to come away with a win somehow. Two Rams took themselves out of the game, exhausted, with twenty-six ticks left. Dick Vermeil, their head coach, couldn't believe it.

As the game clock ticked away, Steve McNair was never better. He hit nine consecutive passes and began moving us down the field. I called the plays and watched the offense execute them perfectly. It was really happening. We worked our way eighty-seven yards in 1:49. On one play, Steve evaded tacklers on an incredible 15-yard scramble. The tackler who finally brought him down got a handful of face mask, and the penalty for that gave us another fifteen yards.

This was all great, but did we have enough clock left? On the second-to-last play of the drive and the game and the season, Steve pulled one more athletic maneuver that kept us alive. There were no open receivers, and the Rams, smelling victory, chased him deep into his own backfield, where a sack would have basically ended the game. Yet with an acrobatic move I never could have coached, he slipped away from two tacklers, kept his balance with a hand on the ground, and shot forward into an opening that provided him just enough space to rifle a 16-yard pass to Kevin Dyson. Two Rams cleverly tried to hold him up and let the clock run out then and there. But Kevin kept his composure. He forced himself to the ground to preserve a few seconds and give us that one last chance. We called time-out.

We were on the 10-yard line. Six seconds left.

Oh, for a few more seconds—for two plays or three. But we had this one shot to work with. This whole season, all the games, all the practices, workouts, and film sessions—and everything would come down to one play and one shot.

Somehow I was calm this time. Against Buffalo, I'd had hope. But I had been a nervous wreck! Now, for some reason, I had never felt calmer. I was the guy who had to set it all in motion—our one chance.

Call a play, Coach.

Biggest call of your life.

They're watching it in Russia.

They're watching it on tiny islands you've never heard of.

This one's for all the marbles. Everything a player or coach or fan dreams about.

This is for the world championship of the game of football.

What's the play?

Coming into any game, a coach does his homework. Coming into a championship game, he does it five extra times. We knew exactly how the Rams would line up in this precise situation—one play left from the 10-yard line. We had reviewed their defensive schemes throughout the season, and on every single occasion without exception they had used the same defensive alignment in this situation. We knew where the corners would be. We knew where the safeties would be; how the linebackers would help on pass defense. I sent in the play.

Gun, spear right, open, zag, firm, sliver, Detroit.

Got that?

Each of those terms told someone in the huddle his assignment. *Gun* meant shotgun. *Spear* identified the basic formation. *Right* was the strong side. *Open* signaled the tight end to split out from right tackle at five yards. *Zag* meant for the wide receiver (Z) to go in motion toward the quarterback, then back to where he started. *Firm* told the offensive linemen what kind of protection to execute. *Sliver* was a slant route inside for the wide receiver, and a vertical route for the tight end. *Detroit* was a combination route on the back side for two other receivers who were split out.

It's not as complicated as it sounds. Each player listens only for the part that he needs.

We had run the "gun, spear right, open, zag, firm, sliver, Detroit" play several times in practice. It called for Kevin Dyson to go six yards downfield and execute a slant route, cutting across the middle into the end zone. Given the alignment we knew the Rams would use, this play would be wide open for six points if Steve could get Dyson the ball.

We had four receivers; St. Louis was in nickel coverage with five defensive backs.

When the ball was snapped, Frank Wychek took off for the end zone. Kevin Dyson slanted to the middle and saw the Rams' Mike Jones turn to cover Wychek. Kevin knew he would be open then. He turned, caught the ball, burst upfield, *and*—

Mike Jones of the Rams, who hadn't lost sight of Dyson after all, turned perfectly and made the tackle of his life. Kevin needed one more step, but Jones wrapped up his legs, making a final surge with the ball impossible.

You can see it on the cover of this book: the most famous tackle in NFL history. As Dyson fell to the ground, his right arm thrust toward the goal line and came down one yard short—even less than that, according to the field judge. Al Jury, who was both judge and jury in this case, signaled "down" and later said the ball was eighteen inches short of the chalk.

Isn't it strange how eighteen inches can define the difference between ecstasy and despair?

Kevin Dyson lay on his stomach, the football still in his hand, and lifted his eyes just in time to see 00:01 roll to 00:00 on the clock. There were Rams leaping and shouting all around him. Mike Jones, a former Missouri fullback who hadn't originally been drafted by any NFL team, was now a celebrity who would make the talk show circuit for the next week.

Some people never get over the kind of spectacular flameout that we experienced at the conclusion of that Super Bowl. Being one yard short can make you crazy. You can spend the rest of your life replaying one moment in time, interchanging all the what–ifs. Our general manager, Floyd Reese, would later say, "You reflect on that play every night, about three o'clock."

The final gun sounded.

It was over. How did I feel? Empty; drained; resigned to the finality of that last play and the final gun. Watching from the press box, I saw the confetti cascading from the roof of the Georgia Dome; Frank Wycheck lying in the end zone, stunned; Jeff Fisher hugging Steve McNair and whispering words of consolation. Those in the press box got up and left without saying a word. I sat by myself for a while, then slowly fought my way downstairs through the crowds and the media. Media people were everywhere, shouting and jostling to ask their questions, most of which were, "Did you make the right call, Coach? Would you change it if you had it to do again?"

I replied over and over again, "It was the right call. We just came up one yard short."

The reporters couldn't get any more out of me than that, and finally they gave up and looked for some other coach or player. I stepped into the coaches' locker room, a quiet and somber place.

Peaceful and Painful

I was calm but empty. I remember the silence of the team as the players showered, dressed, and boarded the chartered buses for the hotel. I was among the last stragglers, sitting in the back of our bus talking quietly with Frank Wychek. He couldn't help thinking that if Jones had taken one more step in his direction, Dyson would have walked into the end zone and we would be celebrating a world championship right now. Mike Jones had simply made the play.

I looked out the window at Peachtree Street, packed with throngs of people enjoying the thrill of a terrific game and a night on the town. I didn't share their joy.

I climbed from the bus and inched my way through the crunch of the crowd toward the long row of elevators. So many people were packed together that it was nearly impossible to move. There was one inescapable thought that I couldn't keep out of my mind: I was the offensive coordinator who called the play that came up short. It was hard not to imagine that every one of these people was aware of that fact: "Hey, aren't you the one-yard-short guy? Nice call!" But in reality, I knew I was just another face in the crowd.

As I looked for an elevator going up, one of the doors opened and Chris stepped off. Our eyes met. Later Chris would tell me, "When I saw your face, I could see the peace in your eyes. And I felt so much better."

Peaceful can still be painful. After getting off the elevator on my floor, I walked back to our room, locked the door, and dropped to my knees. I asked God *why*. Why such a bitter pill for all our players and coaches and fans who had come so far? It seemed that we had pulled out game after game, that we were truly a "team of destiny." Why had we worked so hard and seen so many miracles only to come eighteen inches from the prize; only to be set up for heartbreak? *Why?*

I poured out my frustration, and then I quieted my spirit and *listened*. I was in dire need of an answer from God. After about twenty long minutes of silence, I felt that still, small voice within me.

Les, the team fell one yard short of victory tonight. Do you know how many people out there are one yard short of eternal victory? I expect you to go tell them.

That moment was the most significant for me in my whole Super

Bowl experience; in my whole Titans experience. It was among the most significant moments of my life, for that matter.

Chris and I had prayed particularly hard before this season that God would be glorified by whatever happened. At the time, we had simply needed our team to survive into the postseason so we wouldn't be fired. I knew I would have to learn total dependence on God.

But the prayer was answered in a poignant way that was not so much about my job but rather about his glory. Before the teams had even left the field, Rams quarterback Kurt Warner was speaking into a microphone to an international audience. He had played the game of his life and hit the winning touchdown pass. And now he wanted the world to know he was giving God all the glory. In the days and the interviews that followed, his amazing story came out. Kurt had come into the NFL as a no-name, unwanted, undrafted free agent. He had played arena football and nearly given up the game entirely before turning a corner and becoming a two-time MVP. On top of that, his wife, Brenda, had a testimony that was just as compelling. She, too, was featured prominently by the TV cameras.

Through the most exciting Super Bowl ever, the name of God was glorified in a powerful way.

Playoffs or pink slips. I had known that no matter how hard I worked, there was no guarantee we would make the postseason. I couldn't control the bounce of the ball, the injury of a key player, or the movements of twenty-two men. All I could do was pray that God would care for us. I had to totally depend on him, and he really came through— not just for me. We saw how, in his great plan, so many things worked out to glorify him. Kurt Warner had an opportunity to tell the world about his faith. And now I knew I had a calling to help people claim the greatest victory of all. In a football game, eighteen inches of turf can bring joy to so many people. In eternity, where God's heavens are infinite, how much wider and deeper will our joy be?

The greatest passion of my heart is to help people find out—as many of them as possible. In this life that is no game, I don't want a single person to fall one yard short.

The Extra Point

Have you ever sat in what felt like the ashes of defeat, only to see the situation turned into a victory you never expected?

People have often asked me how heartbreaking it is to lose a close one in the Super Bowl. The truth is that far greater disappointments occur every day in this world, for countless people. For you. For everyone you know. It just happens that no television cameras are there to cover the event . . .

- on that day when your position was eliminated at work,
- on that day when the love of your life walked away forever,
- on that day when the doctor gave you test results that shook your world, or
- on that day when your own child made a decision that broke your heart.

Many of us may face these earthshaking calamities—unemployment, divorce, health crises. As Jesus said, every day brings troubles of its own. The best quarterbacks still miss four passes out of ten, throw a few interceptions, and muff their share of handoffs.

The question is, what goes through your mind on the day of defeat? What were your thoughts the last time you suffered a great disappointment? That's what makes all the difference.

Have you gone from disappointment to devastation to despair? Add one more *D* word: *determination.* Where does it come from?

When the tough times come and you realize that God hasn't stopped working, that's the moment when you begin to turn your defeat into victory. It's easy to be a positive thinker when the sun is shining. But how tough are you when the storm comes full force? Wise people have lived out this rock solid principle:

> Whenever trouble comes your way, let it be an opportunity for joy. For when your faith is tested, your endurance has a chance to grow. So let it grow, for when your endurance is fully developed, you will be strong in character and ready for anything (James 1:2–4).

I'm not suggesting that you walk around with a big grin on the day you lose your job. What I am saying is that in this life of following Christ, nothing is wasted. There are defeats, but good and essential things grow out of them. As James says, the tough times build your endurance, endurance builds character, and then you're ready for anything.

What is the greatest disappointment you've had lately? Could it be that you've already begun to see God working through it? If not, stay tuned. And if you have any doubt that it works—that *God works* through these trials—just keep reading!

3

The Greatest Catch

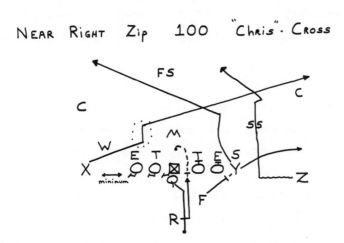

NEAR RIGHT ZIP 100 "Chris"·CROSS

It is autumn of 1971, and the setting is Washington, D.C. The air is crisp and the breeze is cool. Leaves are turning to orange and yellow and brown on the Potomac. Flags are flying—but not the patriotic kind.

It's flag football, and the Senate is taking on the House of Representatives. Add to that the presence of a group of U.S. Marines. It could only happen in our nation's capital.

In those days I was a running back for the Quantico Marines, the national team of the Marine Corps. Our squad didn't play flag football but the real thing. A bunch of the guys had played college ball, and we faced a twelve-game college schedule each fall.

Two of my buddies on the team, Terry Murray and Pete Kimener, were telling me about a flag football league they had found. Sure, it was softer and more informal. But there were girls! It was a coed league that was looking for "a few good men."

Terry and Pete were highly decorated marines. Terry would eventually become a two-star general; Pete would be CEO of a large Midwestern company. In 1971 they were my two best buddies, and it sounded as though they had found a fun way to meet people. One of them was already dating a congressional receptionist on the team. But they needed a quarterback, and they figured I was their guy.

"Oh, I don't know," I said. "I'm still aching from our own game on Saturday."

"Just come and watch," they said. "See what you think."

So I followed my buddies out to the park beside the Potomac River. I stood behind a tree much of the time, peering around it so as not to be too conspicuous. My two buddies were wide receivers. After the game, when they asked my opinion, I told them the team had a receiver who was better than either of them—and it was a girl. We had a good laugh, and they agreed that this young woman, the one Terry called Preppie, was quite an athlete. And of course, they eventually talked me into playing.

These teams were composed of staff members from different House or Senate offices who wanted to play, along with any "ringers" they could recruit to improve their team. Our team was in the House division. The games were competitive, and there was a natural rivalry between the two legislative branches of government. But afterward everyone went out to Georgetown and socialized.

As I joined the squad, we fielded a team of five men and three women. As the new quarterback, I was quick to take charge. In those days, I was extremely competitive, with a drive to be the best at everything in my path. I had a healthy dose of "coach" in me even then. So it wasn't long before I was making up rules, such as the following:

- No giggling in the huddle.
- No planning for after the game during the game.
- If we're going to do this thing, we're going to do it right.

I had no idea the word *social* could apply to football. I always played to win. And to the team's credit, they didn't drop-kick me off the practice field, probably because we began to be pretty competitive. They figured winning was fun, and it let them enjoy the postgame parties even more. Even the good-looking wide receiver known as Preppie put up with Steckel the stickler.

Terry Murray was a native New Jerseyan with Italian roots. He used to put up a little sign in our apartment kitchen that said, "Vito Scarpetti's Galley." He really got a kick out of the whole Italian chef thing. He also enjoyed pressuring me to bring a date to the elaborate Italian meals he fixed on Sunday. One day he said, "Les, why don't you get a date with that Preppie?"

I said, "Who?"

He replied, "The Preppie. You know, our wide-out from Berkeley."

"Preppie, huh?" I laughed.

"Well, call up Preppie and see if she'll come."

As it turned out, the Berkeley wide receiver and I would have to connect on the field before we could connect socially.

I was now playing quarterback, making rules, and drawing up plays, and pretty soon we found ourselves moving up the tournament ladder. Every year, at the end of the schedule, the best team from the Senate would face the best team from the House. It was the D.C. Super Bowl of flag football. Bleachers would be installed, a number of senators and congresspeople would show up, and it would turn out to be quite an event.

Finally, we needed one more victory. If we won this playoff game, we would go to the Super Bowl. So we were focused, hyped, and motivated. The game was tight until, with four or five seconds left, we had our last shot at the victory. I called a play in the huddle. Shotgun formation. It was *always* shotgun formation, by the way, because we had a girl playing center. If you follow football at all, you'll understand the proprieties involved.

So I took the long snap on that final play. I rolled out to the left, looking for my two favorite targets, Pete and Terry, on a crossing route. They were covered.

At the last possible second, I saw a flash of strawberry blond break across the field to my right, frantically waving. It was that good-looking wide receiver—the one Terry called Preppie. Meanwhile, an enemy pass rusher was lunging for my flag. I launched the ball toward the sprinting receiver, but I led her a bit. She stretched out full length, stuck out her left hand, and acrobatically pulled in the game-winning catch, falling into the end zone to score and send us into the championship game.

Naturally, we all went galloping to the end zone to celebrate. I sorted through our pile of players, got to the bottom, and said two things to the good-looking receiver.

The first thing I said was, "Your name again is what?"

The second thing I said was, "Would you like to go out to dinner tonight?"

That was the first pass I ever made at my wife, and it's been love ever since.

East Meets West

In case you're curious, we lost that Super Bowl. But Chris, whom I was now dating, was our MVP. Since then I've been involved in two more Super Bowls, but Prep is still my most valuable partner. I led her on a pass route, and she led me right to the altar.

We think about the chances of it now—our meeting on a football field with American politicos around us—and it seems all the more unlikely. At the time, I was a very conservative U.S. Marine officer from the East Coast who had already completed a tour in Vietnam. Chris, on the other hand, had come from the West Coast and the campus of antiwar Berkeley, where she had decided to major in political science. We came from two different kinds of families, two different sides of the country, two different sides of the political spectrum—though Chris was never really one of those wild campus radicals.

I've always believed that God has a perfect partner for everyone who is destined for marriage. But what happens if the two of them are several worlds away from one another, geographically and otherwise? He is still God, and he finds a way—sometimes a highly unlikely way. I like to think God put his signature on matching us up by having it happen on a playing field. At the time, I had no idea I was heading into coaching as a career. I had no idea where I was heading at all, in fact.

The marine and the Berkeley protester. It sounded like a situation comedy reject, but that's where we found each other, after I found her in the end zone. There would be six of us on triple dates, and Chris would be challenging us, asking questions, sounding us out. I enjoyed her inquisitive spirit and quick mind. But neither of us could have imagined the future that awaited us, either in marriage or in football. I know I was very young, more interested in today than tomorrow, and scared half to death by the very idea of marriage.

After the triple dates were over, Chris and I would talk for hours. She had discovered not only that I was a Christian but that I took my faith pretty seriously. Chris came from a big, tight-knit, churchgoing family, but my spiritual commitment was something new to her. She knew one angle for probing it. "If you're a follower of Jesus Christ and 'Love one another' and 'Turn the other cheek,'" she said, "then how do you rationalize going to Vietnam? How do you balance obeying the military with obeying God?"

Her challenges never upset me. I knew they were good questions. But I also knew there were questions beneath her questions. I smiled and replied, "I don't think your argument is with me. I think you need to take it up with God. Why don't you read this book and ask him these things?" And I gave her a Bible.

Today Chris says that as she fell in love with me, she wondered whether she was falling in love with Jesus. She loved me, I loved Jesus . . . but was the circle complete? Maybe that's why God pulled me away in 1972, all the way to Colorado, leaving the two of them alone to figure out where they stood.

So I was sleeping in an unheated garage in Colorado for eighteen months, taking my first shot at coaching. Chris was traveling back and forth between Washington and California, stopping over to visit me, working on her congressman's campaign, reading that Bible, figuring out whether her relationship with me would survive the distance, and, finally, figuring out whether she would go the distance with Christ.

The answer to both of those questions would be *yes*—for then, for now, for always.

The Girl Next Door

As I got to know more about Preppie and her background, I found myself powerfully drawn to her family. She was and is one of those products of a truly loving household. I've always had reverence for both my parents and the home I came from, and I've always been grateful for the life lessons I learned there. But there were some special dynamics in Chris Pickett's family that I knew I craved.

During her formative years, her dad, Gene Pickett, was always self-employed. He was her hero who encouraged her love of sports. He had played football for the University of California, joined the army, and fought in Italy during the Second World War; we already had a lot in common. He married his high school sweetheart and, returning from the war, started a family—including Chris, her fraternal twin sister, Kathy, their older brother, Mike, and a younger brother, Todd.

Behind the house was the workplace where preserves, candies, and gift packs were created for Gene's business, Markers Kitchen. Workers stirred big copper pots, pitted cherries, and cleaned strawberries as the Pickett children performed musical numbers for the reward of admittance to the candy kitchen. The ultimate privilege, however, was to be able to ride into Los Angeles with Dad to buy the fresh ingredients at the farmers' markets. Chris's mom, Betty May, worked hard and played with equal intensity, whether cards or board games. She made their home fun and full.

It was that kind of 1950s family, not too far from *Father Knows Best*. After we were dating, I would sit in the car in front of Chris's apartment and listen to her family stories for hours, marveling at the love she felt for everyone in that home. I simply hadn't known anyone who could claim such a family or whose face shined so much when she talked about it.

There may have been only one crucial thing that was lacking in that household. One of the great joys of my life was seeing Chris embrace a faith in Christ, then seeing her share it with her parents. Today I would call them a very complete family. Their love was exceptional to begin with, but now the Spirit of God lives in it.

It's not too surprising that Prep emerged from such a solid, healthy environment with strong self-esteem. She brought an energy, an enthusiasm, and a quick wit to all her experiences, built on a foundation of security and self-confidence. Her father made it clear that the future of each of his children was an open book; he would support any direction they chose.

Chris chose the University of Southern California, for starters. Her older brother was there, her twin sister was accepted as well, and she had been offered scholarship assistance. But Cal at Berkeley was an almost irresistible magnet for students interested in politics and government. It was the 1960s then, and even as I was in Vietnam, Prep was transferring to the place where kids were famous for protesting the war.

Chris never became too involved in the unrest and demonstrations. She spent time as a student in Paris. She studied political science. And eventually she followed her heart to Washington, D.C., to serve as a congressional intern. After a summer internship, she landed a job on a congressional staff. In time she became the congressman's press secretary.

And with all the athleticism that ran in her family, she joined a certain flag football team.

I'm really glad about that last part.

"Am I Going to Denver?"

I learned some good things in my family too. One of them was from my dad: *Don't even think about marriage—at least until you're twenty-eight or thirty.* My dad pretty well engraved that law on my brain, and I have to admit I've drummed that same message into my own children and players. My dad's point was that marriage is pretty explosive stuff to play with while you're young and stupid.

So even after Chris and I had been dating for months, I was almost oblivious to that whole subject.

I was driving around D.C. in an old, beat-up Chevy convertible. And I was almost on my way out to my first coaching job as a graduate assistant in Colorado. One day the two of us were in that car when Chris said, "Babe, guess what I've done? I've gotten time off from work so I can ride out west with you and keep you company!"

A warning buzzer sounded off somewhere inside my head. But I didn't say a word; I just turned the car around and headed toward her place in Georgetown.

After a few moments, Chris wanted to know what was wrong. I didn't answer.

I pulled up to her duplex and said, "Get out."

"What?"

"Just get out."

Chris quietly climbed out of the car, tears welling up in her eyes, and walked up the steps to her door. She really didn't understand—who would? I drove around the block with gritted teeth. What Chris had just told me sounded far too serious. It sounded like something approaching the vicinity of the *M* word. Why, she was trying to get her *hooks* into me!

That's what I was thinking as I drove the car in circles. This thing with Chris had been fun while I was in Washington. Now I was off to a new life in coaching. So long, and thanks for the memories! But the buzzer inside my head had been replaced by a voice. It said, "You imbecile! What do you think you're doing?"

After fifteen minutes I was driving up to her duplex again. I apologized, but I had no idea what was behind my actions. It was only later that I realized my fear of marriage. I could stand up to three-hundred-pound offensive linemen, hammer-fisted boxers, and the challenges of Vietnam. But I had my limits!

"I'm really, really sorry," I said.

Chris looked at me and said, "Am I going to Denver?"

I replied, "Yeah. I guess you are."

The Significance of Twenty-eight

Finally, during our long-distance period when I was in Colorado, she broached the subject during a visit. I was driving her back to the

Denver airport when she turned to me and said, "Okay, enough is enough here. What about the future? Are you serious about this thing?"

I knew an ultimatum when I heard one. But I was close to panic. I loved being with Preppie, but I was terribly afraid of marriage. So I pulled the car to the side of the road, under a viaduct. I explained to her that my career was just getting started; that I wanted to get my feet on the ground and build a strong foundation in coaching.

Chris listened patiently and replied, "I'm building my life, too, Les. I'm going to start dating other people as well. As much as I love being with you, if I'm not going to be a part of your future, then that's just the way it is. I need to get on with my own life."

What could I say? Fair enough. For the time being, we kept in touch but also kept our options open—both of us. We both had careers that were in their first stages, and Chris focused on her political world while I investigated coaching football.

At the same time, I was a young man with my share of immaturity. Looking back, I realize the extent to which I was looking out for number one. I had left home for college with a certain rebellious spirit and a controlling personality. Without realizing it, I was on a mission to prove to the world that I was something special. I'd had a couple of close dating relationships, and I saw them as close calls. I simply wanted to have some fun, and the commitment of marriage seemed very frightening to me.

Not much time passed before Chris just happened to take a friend's doctor's appointment. It was Good Friday, and people were heading out for the Easter holiday. Her friend was going to cancel, but Chris said, "I haven't been examined in a while. Let me take the appointment." So she did, and she went through the usual physical exam. The doctor told her that something was showing up—something dark. It might or might not be malignant, but surgery would be required.

Chris flew home and eventually blurted the doctor's news to her family. But far away in Colorado, I had no idea what was going on. I was on a practice field, and I remember feeling a compelling urge to be with Chris all of a sudden. The head coach said he was calling off practices for the Easter weekend. So I thought, *What a great time to make a surprise visit to Chris and her family.* So I got on a plane and headed for California.

I was stopped in my tracks by the news. For the first time, I saw the fragility of life and relationships and the wonderful things we expect to last forever. For the first time I realized Chris wasn't a part of my life I could simply take for granted. As it turned out, she had the surgery and the growth was benign, thanks be to God. But that crisis had claimed my full attention.

It would still be some time before I could pull the trigger on this big decision, but from that moment on I began to take Chris, and my feelings about her, much more seriously. I began to realize that a superficial dating life could never compare to the fulfillment of that one soul mate to have and to hold. As immature as I was, even then I knew that God had a plan for me that included growing up and putting down roots.

The two of us talked a lot less about keeping options open and seeing other people. We gradually moved toward the permanence of marriage. I can remember Mother's Day, talking to her dad on the phone and asking for permission to marry his daughter. I also remember asking Chris to go to two camps sponsored by Fellowship of Christian Athletes. That may seem like a strange request of a fiancée, but by this time I was tied in with that organization's ministry. I wanted Prep to feel the same passion for ministry in the athletic world, so she attended a camp in Delaware and one in Colorado. She came back raving about how great it all was, and by 1975 she was a platform speaker at the first-ever women's FCA conference in Marshall, Indiana.

I turned twenty-eight on July 1, 1974. By my dad's reckoning, I had reached the age of marital accountability. To underscore that milestone, and with my mother's excitement and approval, Chris and I were married on Sunday, July 28. I've now lived more of life married than single, and I couldn't have been more blessed. The Bible tells us there are very special blessings for single people. And there are times when I wonder if football coaching is really better pursued by single men. The demands of the career are unrelenting.

I can remember one of the first games Chris attended as my wife at Colorado. After it was over, she made her way down to the locker room to wait outside for me. Colorado had won the game, so she looked forward to celebrating with me. She saw players, all showered and in street clothes, emerge and go their way. Coaches came out, one by one, along with trainers, the team doctor, and others, all of them laughing and talking about the game and their plans for the evening. The sky grew darker as evening approached. Finally, I came out, and Chris was startled to find me in a surly mood. "What's wrong?" she asked. "We won."

"Yeah, but we didn't play so well," I said. And throughout the course of the evening, I remained moody.

Finally, Chris said, "If this is what you're like when we win, I don't want to be there when we lose."

I can honestly say I took her words to heart. I realized it was unfair to let my wife take the brunt of the pressure of my career, so I have always made certain to be on my best behavior on those evenings following games.

Not that Chris ever struggled with being a coach's wife. She was born for the gridiron. She has accepted every challenge of my career with love and grace and humor. She loves me, but she loves what I do too. There's a significant difference between the two. Preppie is interested in every X and O. She has gotten to know the players. She has loved me through loving my work. This is no small consideration, because often it has meant spending evening after evening alone, or uprooting the family and moving to a new city almost before the boxes were unpacked in the old one. The team colors and the cities and the players have been in constant flux. Through all of it, Chris and the kids and the Lord have been the constants that kept me afloat. Head coaches, general managers, owners, and fans can be fickle—but that inner team of Father and family have never wavered.

The Lord is our strength, but a great part of the armor he provides is the unconditional love of a supportive family. I can't imagine the pathway of my life without that precious gift.

The Extra Point

Early in our marriage, I drew a little criticism from some of the other coaches. I was very young and trying to make a good impression, so this was not a situation I would have sought. But one of them came to me and said, "Hey, Steckel, why don't you ever come to training table with the rest of us?"

Training table is a big deal on football teams. It's a time to make sure the players are eating well while building unity during the meal. On this team, it was an unwritten rule that players and coaches ate dinner together. But what about me? This coach pressed the issue.

I said, "Listen, I'm going to tell you directly. My wife is more important. I have a value system that goes faith, then family, then football. That puts her before training table. I'm sure you understand. Do you see her at practice nearly every night?"

He admitted that he did. It wasn't really usual for coaches' wives to hang out at practice, but Chris would be there whenever she could.

I continued, "Well, after practice, I meet her up on top of the hill for dinner. She brings her Crock-Pot, has something cooked up like stew or soup and sandwiches, and we eat in the car. Then I come to the evening meetings with you guys. I just happen to like being with my wife. I want to work as hard at my marriage as I do at my coaching."

My reasoning was that as long as the head coach himself didn't come to me about something like this, I was on steady ground.

My point is that as Christians, we are a city set on a hill. Jesus said, "You are the light of the world. A city on a hill cannot be hidden" (Matt. 5:14 NIV). I realize that verse says nothing about Crock-Pots on a hill. And to be truthful, Chris and I weren't thinking about Matthew 5:14 as we dined on beef stew. But I came to realize that players and coaches, too, were watching to see what kind of marriage we had. They knew I was a Christian, and my marriage was just about the first place people looked.

I doubt it's any different for you—even if you're not married. What about your significant relationships? Do they shine with light from another world? How do they reflect your beliefs? You've probably seen your share of relationships ruined by the relentless pursuit of career and success. As you'll see, it was only by the grace of God and the love of Chris that I didn't go down in flames—though I came pretty close at times.

Men, approach your marriage as a model for your children and anyone else who is watching. Someday your kids will come behind you and follow your lead. The love, support, and mutual dependence you show them will become a legacy for future generations as they pass it on to their own children.

I mentioned that the people who love you are the armor of God's strength in your life. You'd have to be crazy to go onto a football field without pads and helmet, knowing you were going to face three-hundred-pound giants who can run forty yards in 4.6 seconds. Life off the field is no different. I hope you're not sacrificing the important people around you on the altar of personal goals. Instead, build them up as they build you up.

I've always said that you can lose a few on the road, but you have to win them all at home.

4

So You Want to Be
a Head Coach?

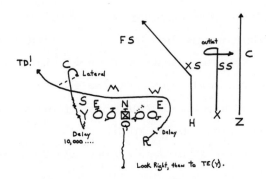

SQUADRON LEFT 50 HOOK & LATERAL

Admit it—you've had dreams of coaching NFL football. You've leaned back on the sofa, closed your eyes, and envisioned yourself stalking the sidelines like Vince Lombardi; guiding your team to championships by playbook brilliance and iron will.

But you've opened your eyes and told yourself, "As if I could ever break into that world! You can't get there from here."

Want to know the truth? Stranger things have happened. For example, there was a 165-pound freshman walk-on at the University of Kansas. He made it through four years of college without ever dressing out for a game—and went on to become one of the NFL's youngest head coaches.

That would be me.

I had some athletic gifts. I played some ball when I was growing up, when I wasn't hustling to work two summer jobs as my dad required. My mother would even chauffeur me at 3:00 a.m. to my job as a garbage collector. There wasn't much time to sleep, much less work out. If athletic fame were required to open the doors to coaching, I would still be waiting.

Then, relatively early in my career, I made it to the top of my profession: head coach of an NFL franchise.

So how did all this come about?

When I was a kid, my sights were set on the service academies. I played high school basketball and baseball, and I was good enough at hoops to be offered a scholarship at Dartmouth. That would have pleased my dad, because he had always dreamed of sending me to an Ivy League school. And pleasing my dad was important to me. But I also wanted to follow his directive always to show integrity in dealing with others. So I told the Dartmouth coach that I saw myself heading to the Naval Academy in Annapolis.

Dad was furious. Mom was in shock. Their point of view was that when opportunity knocks, you throw the door wide open.

My decision looked even bleaker when I couldn't meet the blood pressure requirement that was part of my entrance examination for the Naval Academy. Looking back, I think I was pushing myself even then, and the stress had pushed my blood pressure to the limit. Even after traveling to Philadelphia to take a special test, I couldn't pass that one either. Things looked pretty bleak.

Then the phone rang. "Hi, Les, it's Jim Wesco. Remember me?"

I remembered Jim from the fifth grade in Allentown, Pennsylvania. He had been the kid who came to my desk to thank me for beating up the town bully on my first day of school. I'd had to defend my honor after being ridiculed for having the first name of "Leslie." That event had actually been the beginning of a lot of street fights for me.

Kids were tough in Allentown, and as I was to find out later, brawling was a kind of family birthright on my dad's side.

Jim Wesco. What a surprise to hear from him. He had heard about my failing the physical for the Naval Academy. He offered a few words of consolation as we caught up on the recent events of our lives.

"So what are you going to do now?" asked Jim.

"I have no idea," I said. "The Naval Academy was plan A for me, and I had no plan B."

"Then how about coming out with me to the University of Kansas?"

I replied, "Kansas? Why would I want to go there? Why would *you* want to go there?"

"My uncle is the chancellor at KU. He'll help us both with the paperwork for admission."

I thought it over. "Well," I said, "it's about two thousand miles away, right? Sounds pretty good to me. I'm ready to get away from home."

Ironically, Jim didn't return for his sophomore year. But I stuck it out. I wanted to get my college degree, and I also wanted to play college football. The latter was quite a goal. In those days, the game was different: with no scholarship limitations, major colleges like Kansas had ninety freshmen vying for playing time, then a handful of walk-ons like me. On top of that, my dad had only allowed me to play my senior year in high school, so there was an inexperience factor on my part. I was all of 165 pounds, had no athletic scholarship, no real size, nothing to recommend me but a whole lot of determination.

Learning to Fight

The way the coaches saw it, I was taking up a perfectly good locker and jersey. To scare me off, they put me at defensive tackle my freshman year when we practiced against the varsity. They might as well have placed me on the center line of the freeway. I was consistently steamrolled by bigger guys, and I suppose a lot of guys in my situation were giving up their football dreams. Coaches and teammates were suggesting not too subtly that I do the same. "Why don't you quit, kid?" they would say, standing over me after another collision. They just made me angrier and more determined. I can be very, very stubborn, and my dad had taught me how to stand up and fight for my chances.

That freshman year I was little more than a human blocking dummy on the field. I took abuse every day without a word of encouragement from anybody and tried to be suitably tough on the field. But there were nights when I stuffed my face into my pillow and stifled the rage within me. All I wanted was my chance in a real game. I wanted respect and approval, but I didn't want to admit I didn't have the physical tools at this level.

One negative and one positive perspective came out of that experience. For one thing, I unfortunately discovered how merciless and uncaring coaches can be. They were paid to win, not to play cheerleader to my personal development. For years afterward, this was why I wanted to be anything but a football coach. My view of the profession was not very high.

Second, I developed compassion for the walk-on—the unheralded, uninvited kid who simply wants to compete without the smallest hope of a moment in the limelight. That was me: I persevered for four years without once dressing out for a game. At one point, when I was an upperclassman, I talked the coaches into a partial scholarship. I spent months getting them to agree that I had earned my meal ticket through years on the practice field, helping the starters prepare for games. Finally, they gave in. All summer I hung my hopes on finally receiving some reward, some incentive for all my hard work. But the old coaching staff was fired, and I began my senior year with a new head coach. When I got back to school, he told me he wasn't going to honor that commitment. "There's no scholarship for you," he said, "so I don't know what you're doing here. Why don't you just quit?"

"I'll never quit," I said through gritted teeth.

The coaches rolled their eyes and let me stay. At least they couldn't question my toughness. It was the only weapon I had. The anger inside me began to grow.

One day the custodian of our fraternity walked into my room while I was untying some boxing gloves I'd brought to college from home. "Hey, you wanna come downtown and prove you can use those gloves?" he asked.

"I don't need to prove anything," I said without even looking at him. "I can use these gloves."

The custodian kept after me. "Come on," he said. "We'll go downtown, and you can meet some real boxers."

Finally, I turned to him and asked him what this was all about. "Why do you keep bugging me about going downtown?" I demanded.

What he told me stopped me in my tracks. It turned out that this custodian had a son named Wesley with a gift for boxing. Wesley was going places. He had barely lost a heavyweight AAU split decision to Buster Mathis, one of the greats of that time. Wesley was invited to sign a pro contract, and his dad was glowing with pride. But on the way to that signing, there was an automobile accident. Wesley's leg was broken in three places, and any serious boxing aspirations he had were gone forever.

Wesley's spirit was nearly crushed along with his leg, and his father suffered just as deeply. What he wanted to do now was find some way to turn defeat into victory. He was hustling young boxers on the KU campus, looking for kids for his son to train. Training gave Wesley something to do other than dwell on the cruelty of fate. When I heard his story, I saw the custodian with new eyes. "Sure," I said. "I'll go downtown with you."

The result of this new boxing pursuit was that I got into the best physical condition I've ever been in. I would run three miles to the gym in downtown Lawrence, Kansas, after classes. There I would follow a very strict training routine of skipping rope, hitting the heavy bag, hitting the speed bag, and shadowboxing, each for nine-minute stints. I hardened my stomach with the medicine ball. Then I would spar with another fighter for three rounds. Often this would be someone Wesley's dad had brought off the streets, and in some cases a paroled prisoner—always somebody tough. Finally, I would run all the way back to campus, three miles. I followed this regimen every night.

Two of my training partners went pro, and I might have pursued that career as well, but football was still my top priority. I did enter the regional Golden Gloves competition and won a trophy, going undefeated. But soon enough, it was time for spring football again, and I was back on the football field, a little leaner, tougher, and as angry as ever.

A New Concept

Something else happened during those lonely years in Lawrence, Kansas. One night when I was a sophomore, some of the guys in the frat house were sitting around talking about women, sports, drugs, and all the things college guys talk about. I wandered away and ran into a friend and teammate named Harold Montgomery, who was about six feet five and 265 pounds. "Are you going to hear that speaker tonight?" he asked. I knew the one he was talking about. It was some kind of religious meeting sponsored by a Christian group on campus.

"Not planning on it," I answered.

He said, "Yeah, you are," and redirected me. Harold was a big guy. When he told you what you were going to do, it tended to happen.

The speaker at that meeting talked about life and death. There was something really compelling about him and the way he attacked the subject. I had never faced those issues so squarely. He held his arms out wide and said, "This hand over here is your birth. This hand over here is your death. You don't have anything to do with either one of those events, unless you hold a gun to your head and shoot yourself. And who would call that control? Only God has true control of both."

He looked hard at us and said, "All this stuff in the middle, between the two hands, is your life. Every bit of it is in your control, and Jesus Christ wants that too. He won't take it from you, but he wants you to give it back. If you do that, he will come into your life and his Holy Spirit will live inside you and help you with everything in your life."

I listened to every word. I had never heard anything about making a commitment to Jesus Christ before. To be very honest, I thought that name was a curse word. I had gone to church now and then growing up and sneaked out more than a few times. The concept this speaker laid out was brand new to me. He offered a simple word picture I could understand. But I slipped out of the meeting without taking his invitation.

I thought a lot about that Jesus thing. Not long after that, I walked into a room where a friend named Jim Goodwin was asleep. "Hey, Jim," I said.

He grumbled and turned over.

"Hey, Jim. Remember that guy talking about life and death? The guy in the meeting?"

Jim opened one eye.

I said, "All that stuff, you think it's real?"

Jim said, "Yeah. I think it's real."

It takes me awhile to process a new idea. I thought about it a good bit, and eventually I made the commitment called for by the speaker. I told Jesus I wanted him to forgive my sins. I wanted to accept his gift and let him come into my life, though I understood so very little of what those things really meant.

There was a day on the practice field not long after that when I may have seen the first result of that prayer. A coach was screaming at me as usual. He pulled me right off the field, belittling me and humiliating me in front of all the other guys. In the past this treatment had caused a terrible anger to well up in me, and it was all I could do to suppress it. This time was different. Somehow I felt peaceful, as if it were some other guy the coach was berating. I wasn't angry at the coach this time; instead, I felt rather sorry for him. And then I realized how strange it was for me to have these feelings. Where was this peacefulness coming from? Could this be the Holy Spirit who was described by the speaker at that meeting?

A Second Chance

I graduated in 1968 with a triple major in political science, social work, and human relations. And here I was at another crossroads without any destination in mind. Where to now?

Then there was a phone call from a Marine Corps recruiting officer. The war in Vietnam was escalating, recruiters were working overtime, and there was the enticing lure of football. The officer said, "We have a national football team that travels across the United States and plays twelve games a year against a college schedule. Would you be interested?"

"Wait a minute," I said. "Are you telling me you can be a marine while playing college football?"

"Absolutely."

"But I've used up my eligibility at Kansas."

"Sure, but here's a way to play anyway. In the marines, you get a second chance."

Second chance? A double second chance. I would be going into the military after my missed opportunity at the Naval Academy, and

I would be playing football again. I had a fleeting thought about that commitment I had made to Jesus. Could it be that he cared about me enough to bring me this reward for my hard work?

"Sign me up," I said.

Yet I *still* had to pass that blood pressure test. How was I going to get by that one? Somebody woke me up early in the morning and hustled me away to take a physical. I was nervous because I wanted this new chance so badly. Sure enough, they measured my blood pressure and I was off the chart. So alarming was the reading that the corpsman yelled for the doctor to come quickly.

"You can't kick me out," I said. "You've gotta pass me!" Lots of guys during that time would have been delighted to fail a blood test and miss out on boot camp and Vietnam. But I wanted this thing badly.

Remember, a war was on. The country needed young men. The doctor looked at my score and said, "You pass." There was no explanation, but we all wanted the same thing.

I was quickly en route to Quantico, Virginia, for officer's candidate school and twenty-six weeks of infantry training. I went through The Basic School (TBS), which is part of the experience for every Marine. My Military Occupational Specialty (MOS) was infantry.

The physical and mental challenges of Marine Corps training were beyond my comprehension. The discipline and demand took me to a level far beyond where I could have taken myself. Through thirty-six weeks of intense scrutiny, I evolved from a mind-set of survival to one that gave me the confidence to lead. The word *retreat* is never used in any Marine Corps manual, and defeat is never an option. The training, discipline, and camaraderie I experienced during those early years in the corps will always be some of my fondest memories.

While I kept looking for the football field, my drill instructor didn't seem as interested in that subject as the recruiter had been. "We'll put in a good word for you with the Quantico head coach," they said, "*after* your tour of duty."

Finally, I was off to Vietnam as a second lieutenant. Serving my country was a privilege, and I'll always be grateful for the opportunity. Like everyone who served in the war, I had an adventure that expanded my horizons and helped me along on the road to maturity.

The U.S. Marine Corps had six security positions in Vietnam: Quang Tri, Hue, Da Nang, Hoi An, Tam Ky, and Quang Ni. Congressmen, generals, VIPs, and other visitors to the war zones often needed an escort to one of these six locations, and I was the officer responsible for providing security so they could get in and out safely. We protected the command posts in these six areas.

Here I was, a second lieutenant at the ripe old age of twenty-three, responsible for two hundred fifty Marines and eighty Vietnamese soldiers who had been assigned to me. I was given a helicopter with warrant officers as the pilots, and we were constantly in the air, moving from operation to operation.

I will never forget one moment when I believed I was on my way to meet my Maker. It was during the monsoon season. We were flying north toward Quang Tri in a small Huey chopper, with two pilots. I was sitting in the backseat on the end, with two other marines. We always flew with both sides of the chopper open, and I could feel a powerful breeze blowing through one side and out the other.

The rain was coming down as we flew along the shoreline, which was lined by a mountain ridge. We were rounding one side of the mountains just as another chopper came around from the other side, precisely in our path. We could see the startled faces in the other copter, as if we were flying into a mirror. One of the soldiers beside me instinctively dove to the door, bailing out. He came right across my lap, and I snagged him by the back of his pants and held on tight. At the last possible second, the other copter went down and we went up. It was a terrifying near miss.

The oddest element about that memory is that we never spoke. When we landed at Quang Tri and unloaded, still no one said a word. We lived every day with the knowledge that copter crashes were as common as breakdowns on the freeway in America. There would be reports of guys with whom you went through basic training, guys who had now lost life or limb. Death was always at your elbow, but you stayed immersed in your own world and your own assignment. I learned the solid fact that is with me to this day, that whether I lived or died was not in my hands.

Gid Adkinson was a Christian I met who liked studying his Bible. We shared verses and faith and encouragement. I felt God's presence many times as a marine far from home, and I began to learn what it meant to depend on him and to trust him for another day of life. Just staying alive can't be taken for granted in a war zone.

I made a resolution that if God brought me home, I was going to do something special for him someday.

Into the Revolving Door

After my tour, I came back to the States. I was back in Quantico playing football and crossing paths with Chris. So many things in my life came together in that brief period. Vietnam provided an accelerated school of learning, and I was ready to see what came next in life.

The course of study that had really captured my heart at Kansas was human relations. I'd had the idea of becoming a social worker and counseling gang members in New York City. There was just something inside me that was drawn to helping young people get moving in the right direction. At Quantico, I had started a Sunday school class so I could teach teenagers who lived on the base. That class went very well—the kids loved it, and their parents were grateful. Some of my friends were beginning to say, "Les, you're a natural teacher, and you love football. Shouldn't you be taking a look at coaching?"

My consistent answer: "No way." As far as I was concerned, it was the last job in the world for me. But my friends kept arguing that a coaching position would be a perfect fit. And there was no doubt about my love for football.

If you can believe it, I had to decide between coaching and Richard Nixon. I was there in Washington as a marine interviewing for various jobs, and somehow my name came up with recruiters for CRP, the Committee to Reelect the President. The 1972 campaign was getting into swing, and of course history records it as the one that led to the Watergate scandal. I went in for an interview and answered some questions from two men. They wanted someone to travel around the country and work on getting out the youth vote.

The voting age had just been dropped to eighteen, so there was a lot of speculation about the effect that all those new young Baby Boomer voters would have on elections. I was a marine and a football player, a clean-cut guy. I got a second phone call and was offered a job making $28,000 per year. That was an impressive salary in the early seventies for a young guy just coming off active duty. But I wasn't sure. I can remember calling my dad on the phone and telling him about these two options. On the one hand, there was the campaign job. On the other, I could be an assistant coach, a graduate assistant for $150 per month.

My dad said, "Are you out of your mind? You're looking at $150 a month versus $28,000 a year, and you need me to tell you what to do?" And he slammed down the phone.

Well, he was right. Consider the dollars, and there was no comparison. I knew it came down to one question: *Do you want to be a football coach?* That meant a sweaty locker room, starvation wages, an obscure slot among sixteen other grad assistants. (Some people have a hard time believing there could be sixteen graduate assistants on one football staff. But it was true. In the seventies, there was no limitation to the number of assistants a college team could use.)

Chris and my marine buddies had nudged me into taking a trip to Hollywood, Florida, for the American Football Coaches Association Convention. It was a bold move, considering I was deeply uncertain about my direction. I attended the convention and probably stood out like a hockey puck under a goal post, a young marine in a sea of career football people. I could see that these folks enjoyed their profession. I was intrigued by their passion and wanted to investigate further.

I stood around, handed out résumés, and tried to make connections. It's a challenge to be a young guy trying to get a foothold in a new world. I had nothing to recommend me but my character and my willingness to withstand rejection. This is what you do if you want to become a coach. You go where the coaches gather. You work the network, talking to everyone you know who knows someone who knows someone. You send out letter after letter, politely requesting an opportunity, changing the addressee each time—University of Idaho, Illinois, Iowa. Chris helped me type them all. Then when you're presented with an opening, you climb in at the entry level and pay whatever dues need to be paid. In our business that means being a graduate assistant on a college team, nominally a grad student but coaching full-time hours for part-time salary: in my case, maybe $150 per month at the University of Colorado. That was the school that finally gave me an offer.

Rookie Coach

I moved to Boulder, Colorado, and spent a year as a graduate assistant, sleeping on a cot in an unheated garage. I found immediately that even at the entry level, I enjoyed a lot of elements of this new world. There was the camaraderie with other coaches—working out, playing basketball, digging into the mechanics of football and the art of teaching it. In that first year of 1972, I stood on the sideline as a graduate assistant while the Colorado Buffaloes played the Oklahoma Sooners on national television. That was my first exposure to just how big this game could be. The excitement and emotion I felt captured me.

I was three years older than the other grad assistants, and I was a marine, so the head coach gave me some preferential treatment. He allowed me to participate in staff meetings, for example. Yes, I was beginning to like this coaching thing. Maybe it was the career for me after all.

I moved up to a full staff position as a receivers coach the following year. It was 1973, and Colorado was the consensus preseason national champion. I couldn't wait for the games and the chance to be part of a powerhouse team. But two weeks before camp, our quarterback coach was fired. Our star quarterback immediately quit the team in protest. It was one of those years. We didn't win the national championship—we lost six games and the head coach and his staff were let go. Just as I saw how great it all could be in 1972, I saw how quickly it could turn around in 1973. The ball can bounce the wrong way a couple of times, and your career takes a hit. It didn't matter. I was hooked on coaching football by this time. But with the hiring of a new head football coach, my future at CU was uncertain.

However, Bill Mallory, a great new coach from Miami University in Ohio, retained me as the only holdover from the old staff. Bill and Ellie Mallory modeled the life of a coaching family in a way that would have a huge impact on us. Their devotion to each other and their concern for the families of the staff would never be forgotten. They now have three sons in the coaching ranks. It's definitely the family business.

I needed that kind of influence because I still had some growing to do. I have to be truthful and admit that I was impatient, driven, and overly ambitious in those days. Once I decided I'd found my profession, it was all about climbing to the top as quickly as possible. So I pushed people hard. I criticized. I clashed with other coaches at times. When we played pickup basketball games, I always thought, *You don't want to play one-on-one with Les Steckel. You don't know how badly I want to win.* I knew deep down that I wasn't approaching people the right way. Having been raised by two parents who were hard-driving perfectionists, I was one myself. Excellence wasn't enough when it came to the players I coached; flawlessness was all I would accept.

One rather embarrassing example involved a player we had at Colorado named Rick Elwood. There was a lot of excitement about him when he came into the program because he was exceptionally gifted as an athlete. He was a full-speed kind of guy, but he lacked toughness. I used to ride him hard about being "soft." One day during spring ball, I told him to meet me at the field house for extra training. He replied, "Coach, that's a day off for the players." I told him to be there anyway.

I got there early and requested a couple of helmets and a set of shoulder pads from the equipment manager. I went to the team meeting room, where I moved all the benches against the wall, clearing the middle of the room, and locked the doors. When Rick arrived to find me in helmet and pads, he had that deer-in-the-headlights look. "Dress out," I said. "Then stand against that wall. I'll stand against the other one. You're going to come running and knock me down. Give me your best shot."

"Really? But, Coach . . ."

"I'm serious. Let's see how tough you are."

We hit, and hit, and hit until we were both covered with sweat and even bleeding a little. After it was over, we sat on a bench to catch our breath. I said, "Rick, the reason I did this is because you can be a really great player. I know you've noticed I like my receivers to be the toughest, most hard-nosed players on the field."

It all went along with the overzealous, gung ho marine image I was trying to live out. I was going to be the toughest guy out there and have the toughest players. As it turned out, Rick and I became great friends over the years, as silly as my demonstration was. He actually made it to the NFL and played for the Broncos for a short period. We still talk occasionally—without the helmets and pads.

I worked with Bill Mallory for three years before leaving to coach at the Naval Academy with George Welsh in 1977.

The League

Being part of the rich army-navy game tradition was one of the great experiences of my life. I wish every coach could be a part of it for one season.

While I was coaching in Annapolis, I met a Washington Redskins assistant named Pete McCulley. His son played for the Naval Academy, and one day Pete visited a spring practice and watched us work on the field. As a receivers coach in the NFL, he told me he was impressed with the top draft choices I had coached at Colorado—players like Don Hasselbeck and Dave Logan. When he became the head coach of the San Francisco 49ers the next season, he called and offered me a job.

After a short apprenticeship in my profession, I was on my way to coach in the NFL at the age of thirty-one. I was hired to coach tight ends and wide receivers. It was another period when life seemed to shift into the next gear. Just a few seasons ago I'd been a graduate assistant on a college team. Now I'd made it to the league, and we were going to be parents—Chris was expecting our first son at this time.

As a young man with a job in the NFL, I sometimes thought it was odd to be coaching players my age and older. That year with the 49ers, I coached O. J. Simpson in his final season. After many seasons with the Buffalo Bills, Simpson finished out his career in his hometown of San Francisco. I happened to be coaching the running backs, because the former coach of that position had become the interim head coach when the owner fired our head coach just nine weeks into the season. With a smaller staff that season, only two of us—Mike White and I—were coaching the offense. I worked with Steve DeBerg at quarterback and with Freddy Solomon and Gene Washington at receiver, as well as with the tight ends.

As my responsibilities shifted to different positions, I was learning a lot about football—and I knew it. My confidence was building, and with it a fair share of arrogance. I wanted more responsibility, more opportunity, and more attention. That's the way it is with driven people. After sleeping on a cot in an unheated garage in my early days in Boulder, now I could see my name in the newspapers. Large crowds came to see our practices at training camp, and there were private hotel rooms, chartered flights, banquet-sized meals, and higher salaries. Our games were televised every week. Yes, it became easy for an immature young man to begin to believe he was something special. Of course, no coach gets that idea for too long before the inevitable firing brings him back down to earth.

I learned about losing my San Francisco job over the radio while I was driving home from work. The organization was cleaning house. The NFL had been exciting while it lasted. I went into the off-season looking for the next opening, painfully aware of the coaching truism that if you don't have a job by March 1, you don't have a job. And I was in a particularly tenuous position. NFL teams looked upon me as having only one year of experience; college teams looked upon me as someone who would run back to the NFL at the first opportunity. So I wasn't a hot property on either side.

Do you want to be a football coach? This is the time when you wonder—Christmas, January, February, watching the phone and missing those NFL perks. How could you have taken the good life for granted? One minute you're in the league, one of the elect, and the next minute you're wondering if you're headed for some other line of work: auto sales or life insurance. You pace up and down the hall, driving yourself and your family crazy. Chris and I would put Christian, our newborn son, in the stroller and take long walks on Fisherman's Wharf. We explored the City by the Bay just to fill our days.

On to Minnesota

One day we were heading out the door for that purpose when the phone rang. Chris picked up the receiver, and her eyes grew large. She began to stutter like Porky Pig. "It's Bu-Bu-Bu-Bu . . . It's Coach Grant!"

Chris knew who Bud Grant was. Everyone did. He was one of those NFL names; one of those walking institutions; one of those franchise builders like Lombardi, Brown, Landry . . . and Bud Grant. When you thought of the Minnesota Vikings, his face came to mind. He was one of those people I studied and imitated.

I grabbed the phone and said, "Who is this, really?"

"It's Bud Grant."

I wasn't certain. Some wise guy could have been pulling a prank. But eventually Coach Grant calmed me down and broke it to me that he had a position to talk with me about. He wanted to see me on March 7.

"Coach, I have a commitment on March 7."

"Can you break it?"

For Bud Grant, you can break it.

On March 7, six days after my old salary ran out, I flew to Minnesota to interview with Bud Grant. It went well, and toward the end Bud asked me if I had any questions. I told him I had only two. The first was whether my wife could attend practices. He had never been asked that one, but he said it would be no problem. What was that second question?

"Coach, why do you go to training camp so late? The Vikings

report eight days before the first exhibition game, while other teams are in camp four, five weeks ahead."

Bud Grant answered the question without blinking. "Les, they don't hand out the trophies in the beginning."

Grant was a successful coach, and as he saw it, there was no need for overkill when it came to practice. It worked for him, and you have to wonder if he had a point. This generation is prone to overwork when it comes to career and competition.

I settled into my job coaching receivers, tight ends, and special teams. I was the eager rookie on a veteran coaching staff. These men had been together as a staff for years. But the coach seemed to see something in me and took me under his wing. We'd be on a plane or a team bus, and Coach Grant would say, "C'mon, Les, sit here," beckoning me to the seat on the aisle beside him. He opened up with me more than was usual for him. I was also close to Jerry Burns, the offensive coordinator and one of the funniest people I've ever been around. And a handful of seasons passed by in a positive way.

Hook, Lateral, Squadron

A career highlight moment came in 1980 when the Vikings were playing the Cleveland Browns. It was the next-to-last game, and both teams had to win to go to the playoffs. Cleveland was trying to win the AFC Central, and we were trying to win the NFC Central. So the game itself had a playoff atmosphere. It was the last game of the season in old Metropolitan Stadium, so it was outdoors and very cold. The game was tight, and near the end of regulation the Browns had a lead when they punted the ball out of the end zone with only a few seconds of play left. Their kicking team came off the field celebrating. Our part of the sideline (both teams stood on the same side of the field at the old Met) was completely dead, gloomy. The Browns were all but headed for the postseason, because we had eighty yards to go in about fourteen seconds.

In those days I wasn't in the press box but down on the sidelines. We had one emergency "must win" type of play we had run just a few times in practice, and I was reviewing it with the players. You may not believe this, but I was tracing it in the dirt with a stick, because the ink had frozen in our pens. It was that cold. This play was a "hook and lateral," though no one had ever run it quite the way we had it drawn up. At the snap, the tight end would pause to let the line-backer drop deep. Ted Brown, our running back, would come out of the backfield and cross the other direction. Joe Senser, the tight end, would run a hook route; Senser would catch the ball from the quarterback and turn and lateral to Brown, who should be all alone; and Brown would be off to the races. Fun, right?

I was standing next to stoic Bud Grant on that cold sideline in the waning seconds. Coach Grant spoke to Jerry Burns, the offensive coordinator, up in the booth: "Okay, Jerry, whaddaya got?"

Jerry, in his usual uncensored style, replied, "Run Les's —— play."

Coach Grant said, "Seriously, Jerry. Whaddya got?"

Jerry repeated, "Run Les's —— play."

I said, "Relax, Coach, it's going to be okay." Bud Grant was not known for wild, high-risk football.

Coach Grant called Les's —— play. Ted Brown came running up to me. "Coach, Coach," he said. "You sure you want me to delay coming out of the backfield?"

"Yes, the play won't work unless you delay it," I said. "You've got to give it time to develop." Brown ran onto the field.

The play was run just right. Ted Brown moved into position like a stealth jet, with nobody picking him up. The defense converged on Joe Senser, who flipped the ball to Brown. Brown took off down the sidelines, but he knew he'd never make it all the way. With just a couple of seconds on the clock, Ted Brown—one of the smartest players I ever worked with—stepped out of bounds once he passed midfield to preserve time for one more play. On the next play, we called Squadron All Go, which sent our receivers downfield for the classic "Hail Mary" tip play. Ahmad Rashad leaped for the ball when it was tipped, somehow kept both feet in bounds, turned, twisted, fully extended an arm, and brought in the football with a single hand. He toppled into the end zone, and we won the game. That was one more NFL classic in which I was proud to have participated. It's still remembered as one of the greatest plays in Vikings history.

Reaching the Top

In 1983 the University of Minnesota approached me about their head coaching position. Those two words were the biggest in my galaxy at that time: *head coach.* It's the dream of all career assistants—wondering what they could do if they were the ones calling the shots; if they were given a team, a staff, a shot at greatness.

By 1982 the lure of the profession had me so fully in its grip that I became obsessed with becoming a head coach. I thought that nothing less could satisfy my soul. It was my last thought before going to sleep every night: *When will I get my chance? When will I get my own team?* I was completely unconscious of my own drivenness. I only knew that I couldn't sleep; my mind was working all the time. And so, one night in late 1983, I gave up on the prospect of slumber. I rose from bed, walked into my study, and dropped to my knees beside the window. A huge harvest moon looked down on me from the night sky.

I prayed, "Lord, I'm scared to death. This head coaching thing is all I can talk about, all I can think about, everything I've dreamed about. You know what's inside me, Lord; you know me better than I know myself. Tomorrow they're going to make the offer. I want it, but I don't know if you want it for me."

I paused and had a crazy thought. "Lord," I said, "let something fall out of the sky. I just need a clear answer. Please, let something fall out of the sky to tell me what to do."

A few hours later I left for work. And at the end of the day, Bud Grant materialized in my doorway—something that didn't happen too often with assistants. He said, "Les, can I see you for five minutes?"

The word was out about the college job. Reporters knew, players were asking me if I was leaving, and I figured Bud had the same question. I was in for a shocker.

He said, "Les, I understand you're going to be offered the job at the university. We respect you a great deal as a coach and as a person, and I want you to know one thing. I'm going to retire at the end of the season, and I want you to be my successor. The general manager and the owner agree with me. We want you to be the next head coach of the Minnesota Vikings."

When I got home, Chris asked, "So what happened today?"

I said, "Something really big fell out of the sky."

We had two small children and another one on the way—just a typical young family, yet I was going to be the second-youngest head coach in NFL history up to that time. I was thirty-seven years old. Only Don Shula had made it to the top faster. Chris and I wanted to call everyone we knew—and maybe everyone we didn't know. We wanted to shout it from the Minneapolis rooftops. But we had to stifle our excitement for three months, until the end of the season when the club could get everything in order and Bud would make his decision public. That made it awkward for me to tell the athletic director at the University of Minnesota that I couldn't come after all.

Jerry Burns came running into my office the next day. He had run interference for me on the college job, really singing my praises to his friends at UM. Now the word on the street was that I was turning it down. He couldn't understand it. UM had put a fantastic offer on paper. He blurted, "Can't you —— read?" It was hard not to tell him, but I was a marine—name, rank, serial number only. I knew how to keep a secret. Jerry Burns went back to his office and made another recommendation to his friends at the university. He called an old graduate assistant of his named Lou Holtz. Holtz went on to great success at Minnesota, at Notre Dame, and at other schools.

But people around the university were upset with me. The way they looked at it, I had suddenly backed out after all the wheels were turning, and I had placed them in an embarrassing position.

I felt terrible about it, but there was nothing I could do. Besides, God had worked all this out, hadn't he? The future couldn't shine more brightly. After all, it hadn't been long since I was walking around wide-eyed at the coach's convention in Hollywood, with no credentials, no experience, just standing there on the outside looking in. Now we had an opportunity beyond our dreams. I had never thought I had any shot at being head coach of an NFL team. It meant something to be admitted into a fraternity that included Tom Landry and Chuck Noll and Don Shula.

Where the Wind Blows Hardest

So there we stood at the summit. More than ever, I wanted to be a football coach. Now my sights were set on championships . . . Super Bowls . . . For years I had been possessed by drive and ambition, and now I poured all my accumulated determination and energy, everything I had, into this opportunity.

I poured too much.

I discovered that the wind blows hardest at the top of the mountain. No matter how fast your climb, the fall can come in the blink of an eye.

If you were a football fan in 1984, you may have tuned your television to CBS one Sunday afternoon. *The NFL Today* was coming on, with Brent Musburger, Irv Cross, and Jayne Kennedy. In their witty style, they presented a short segment about the crazy happenings up in Minnesota, former kingdom of the stoic Bud Grant. As Brent and Irv told it, the franchise had fallen into the hands of a crazy marine, some kind of cross between GI Joe and Yosemite Sam from the Bugs Bunny cartoons.

They had the films to prove it. CBS blared the Marine Hymn as they showed me trotting onto the field, then doing the obstacle course with the team. I was the new sheriff in town—the hard-charging, gung ho marine. It made a great story and set up a few jokes. I have to admit I played right into this perception. I loved the boot camp angle, and I said, "Let's have some fun with this thing."

I also brought in some military training philosophies, such as having the Seabees build us an obstacle course. The Vikings wouldn't pay for it, so I called the boys from the navy and they put one in over the weekend. The front office folks came in Monday morning, and there it was, the obstacle course I had described, as if it had dropped out of the sky. They couldn't believe their eyes.

I created an Iron Man conditioning program and competition that frankly was a few years ahead of its time. The players resented it deeply. Then I brought in drug testing, which was not required in those days. Peter Ueberroth, baseball commissioner and Olympic chairman, later called me the pioneer of drug testing in sports. There was great resistance to such requirements, even from the league. A lot of denial was going on, and coaches wanted to pretend there was no problem. But I pushed for drug testing and angered a lot of our guys.

I was young, reckless, naive, and in just about everybody's face. I was eager to change every detail I could lay my hands on. And I was not too subtle in the way I went about handling people and situations. I ran a preseason camp that was more like a military boot camp, and it shook up the system after Coach Grant's less strenuous style. I rode the players hard—far too hard, really.

I demanded perfection and accepted absolutely no excuses. One day three players were late for a team meeting. As they walked in, I yelled at them in front of everybody. "You're late and you're fined," I said.

"Coach," said one of them, "we were actually stuck in an elevator. It just stopped between floors and there was nothing we could do. You can check with the people in the building, and they'll tell you—"

I wouldn't even let them finish. "I don't care! It's your job to be here."

"Are you going to fine us?" asked one of them incredulously.

"Yeah, you were late. Sit down!"

The room was very silent. The disapproval of the team was almost tangible, but I didn't care. I was caught up in that crazy marine image, and in my own mind I couldn't be wrong. In this case, the players were right and I was wrong. They needed discipline, but I applied it in all the wrong ways.

I had problems with the other coaches as well. The front office had required me to keep the old staff—to be loyal to Bud's guys. These were friends and colleagues, my elders who had helped me grow into NFL coaching. But I was seen as Bud Grant's fair-haired boy. I had passed them by. The management patted me on the back and said, "Bide your time. At the end of the season, you can bring in your own people." But I brought in a few of my own anyway and shifted some of the existing coaches to less meaningful positions. I was insensitive and failed to use the human relations skills that my college major had been all about.

Some of the players had been kept on past their prime. Bud Grant was always loyal to his personnel, and as a result we had a number of athletes who weren't at their best. Then our top draft choice and several of our other draftees were hired away by a new and short-lived league called the United States Football League (USFL). Our five highest-paid players were all injured and out of action. On top of that, we sent player after player to nearby Hazleton, to a drug treatment center, right in the middle of the season. Reporters would ask where this player or that one was, and we would simply say, "He is attending to a personal problem."

But add up the injuries, the treatments, the lost draft choices, the friction on the staff, and my reckless immaturity, and it's easy to see how we stumbled to a 3–13 season. And a once-popular assistant was now a hated head coach. The same players who had loved me came to resent me overnight. A local sports reporter, trying to earn his stripes, entered our locker room and polled the players about reasons they disliked me. I cut off his questioning, and the media became even more hostile.

"Like John McKay"

No tough times are without a few nice moments. I remember one of our few victories, this one against Tampa Bay. John McKay, their original head coach, was still with them then. He had been the coach at Southern Cal when Chris was a student there, so he was her first great model of what a head coach was all about. Years before, on the day when I had told her I was thinking about becoming a coach, we were in my car. I made my announcement, and she quickly slid over to my side of the front seat, gave me a tremendous hug, and said, "You mean like John McKay?"

Now I was going head-to-head against him. It was a close game late in the fourth quarter, and we were driving down the field. We needed a field goal to win. I always had a philosophy about when to send in my kicker. I needed to know that the kicker wanted the ball. Nothing good comes from sending him in there when he's not sure he can make the kick. So I was going to keep calling offensive plays until the kicker convinced me he wanted that kick. The great Jan Stenerud, the only kicker in the NFL Hall of Fame, was our kicker that year.

With a handful of seconds left, we were within distance of a long field goal—not a sure thing. Jan ran over and said, "Les, what are you doing? Call time-out so I can go in and win this game!" That's what I like to hear. I called it; he kicked it; we won it. After the game, I gave the game ball to Chris since she was such a McKay fan. As tough as that season was, she earned it.

But the gloomy moments outnumbered the cheerful ones. By the grace of God, it was all over after a year. Chris and I turned to our faith, our home Bible study friends, our church, and our family. We tried to keep everything in perspective. Our kids Christian and Lesley brought us great joy, and Luke was on the way. His advent was a solid reminder to us of the future—something to cling to when the present is bleak.

To this day I offer my deepest apologies to the players and coaches who were bruised during my learning experience. The morning after our season-ending loss to Green Bay, I was called in and asked for my resignation. I wouldn't do that, because I had drilled it into my players never to quit. So I had to be fired. Bud Grant returned to coach for one year as part of a lifetime contract with the organization. And thus I became the answer to one of the popular NFL trivia questions, "Who was the Vikings head coach between Bud Grant and Bud Grant?"

I wasn't finished quite yet, though I couldn't help asking myself that question again. I had to ask it as the TV vans and reporters, and all their flashes and wires and microphones, camped on my lawn the day I was dismissed. As all the commotion spilled across our lawn and frightened our children, I had to ask myself, "Do I want to be a football coach?"

And miraculously, I did. But I had to learn something about myself the hard way. As the years have gone by, Chris and I have thought a lot about the year 1984. We've come to the conclusion that God front-loaded my career for a good reason—just to get that head coaching stuff out of the way early, because it wasn't his plan for me. The only way I could understand that was for him to give me what I wanted and let me stumble. Good parents have to do that with their children occasionally, though they hurt with us.

Sometimes God leads you up to the mountaintop, where the wind can almost knock you down. He shows you the Promised Land spread out before you. Then he turns, looks you right in the eye, and asks, "Are you certain this is what you really want?"

For years, my mantra was, *I want to be a head coach!* I talked about it, prayed about it, obsessed over it. Then God let me see with my own eyes and feel with my own heart that what I want is not always what I need. Through his grace and mercy, he allowed me to shatter that false god early enough in my career so I could become a little wiser and begin to rethink my life and my maturity.

Not that I had all the answers yet—you'll see that in the next chapter. But the Vikings experience helped me understand that there were areas of my life that needed a little seasoning, a little time for maturing. And like all trials, this one drove me more toward the Father who consoles and encourages us just when we need it most.

The Extra Point

If I could x-ray your heart and soul today, what dream would I find lurking there? Would it be something like owning your own business, making a million, living in a dream house? There's nothing wrong with heartfelt desire, as long as we realize that only God can quench our deepest thirst and fill our deepest hunger.

God certainly gave me my dream, but I was like the dog chasing the car: I didn't know what to do with it once I caught it. What about God's dreams for you? I know people who are afraid to find out what he wants because they assume it will involve the missionary life some-where across the world.

But here is the terrific part: God begins with the dream, then builds you to fit it. Whatever it is he wants for you, you can be certain that it will bring you joy like nothing else could. I'm a living testimony of that fact. As I've followed the path of learning God's plans for me, things have just grown better and better. The real dream for any of us is this: serving him exactly the way he designed us to serve him. We have a dream; he has a plan.

Today I challenge you to take hold of this incredible promise from the Scriptures: "'For I know the plans I have for you,' says the LORD. 'They are plans for good and not for disaster, to give you a future and a hope'" (Jer. 29:11).

Imagine a great blueprint laid out on God's table. It's the blue-print for your life, and he has created it with the same perfection that he used when he made the mountains and the galaxies. This plan shows every stage of your life, from school to family to career to serv-ice. These are plans for your good, to bring you a future and a hope.

Don't you know that finding and following the Master plan is the greatest adventure you could ever undertake? Therefore, why not spend a little extra time in prayer today, asking him to help you make sure you're moving in the right direction?

Begin by following your dream, because it's the leading indicator of exactly how God designed you. But as you follow, be on the look-out for that place where your dream merges with his plans. That, my friend, is the most important landmark of your life. It took me years to learn it, but that one lesson made all the difference.

5

The Father Factor

JUMBO I RIGHT TITE 12 ISO

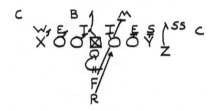

Tough times offer a hidden gift: they drive us to the counsel of the wise.

We don't listen nearly so well when things are going our way. But adversity begets humility. We come to the painful realization that we don't have all the answers or ability we may have thought. The voice of experience is suddenly worth hearing.

Looking back on the aftermath of 1984 and the Vikings, I realize how God spoke through wise older servants. I also realize how decisive were their words in helping me begin to understand what was inside me. For example, there was Tom Landry, who invited me to visit his home. For me, that was like a trip to the White House.

Landry, of course, was another NFL patriarch—an American icon.

The Dallas Cowboys were America's team, and Landry, with his old-school hat and grimace, had always been their coach. He was as stoic as Grant, as successful as Lombardi, and also a very devout Christian.

After the seasons of 1982 and 1983, he had asked permission of the Vikings to interview me for a job, but the Vikings had declined. I was deeply disappointed because I naturally gravitated toward Landry. I wanted to learn all that I could, and he embodied football, faith, and fatherhood to me.

Sitting in Landry's living room was therapeutic. He was quiet, thoughtful, consoling as I poured out my disappointment and regrets. I knew that he cared about me, and I harbored every hope that someday I could serve on his staff. Coach Landry said, "Les, I want you to know that I was very fortunate in the way my coaching career began. You actually won more games in your first season than I did in mine. You won more than Chuck Noll of the Steelers did, for that matter. But here's what happened to me. The media and the fans were giving us a hard time. Tex Schramm called Clinton Murchison Jr., the owner, and said, 'We're going to have to respond to the uproar somehow.' Mr. Murchison said that he would sleep on it and get back to them.

"Well, after a few days Mr. Murchison called Mr. Schramm back and said, 'Here's my response: let's give Tom Landry a ten-year contract, because I know I have the right man.' "

Coach Landry concluded, "Les, not everyone is as fortunate as I was. You've just got to hang in there and trust God to lead you toward what he has next for you."

I was told that Coach Landry rarely invited coaches or players to his home. Regardless of how common it may have been, it was a wonderful comfort in my life. I felt angry and rejected, and here was one of the men I respected most, reaching out to me and encouraging me, even letting me know he was interested in hiring me at some point.

But another mentor did even more to heal my wounds during this period. His name was Raymond Berry.

I had first come to know Raymond when I was a young coach learning the ropes at Colorado. The phone rang one day, and it was a name I knew—a guy who coached receivers for the Cleveland Browns but, more important, an NFL Hall of Fame receiver who had caught passes thrown by Johnny Unitas. Raymond Berry was a good athlete but a great preparation guy; someone who watched hours of game film and walked every inch of a playing field to find dips and rough places—anything to give himself an edge on his pass routes.

Raymond's obsessive attention to detail impressed an ambitious rookie coach like me. He was calling me to ask about some Colorado receivers, but in later calls I did the questioning. I wanted to know everything I could about pass routes and other fundamentals of being a receiver.

In 1984, when I was a head coach, I asked Raymond to help me on a consulting basis in my old position of coaching receivers. Bud Grant had counseled me not to try to replace myself in that area, because I had a special bond with our receivers. I wanted Raymond to come in just for training camp, to help our guys get going. I knew it would be good to start my head coaching career with a respected friend at my elbow. He came, he kept an eye on me as a coach, and he kept an eye on me as a person—even though I was unaware of it at the time.

Then, halfway through the 1984 season, the New England Patriots brought in Raymond as their interim head coach. It was an unusual situation, because in most cases a team will play out the season before firing and hiring. And bringing in an outsider like Raymond was an even more striking move for a team like the Patriots. But it worked for them. And by the end of that season, I was on my way out in Minnesota; he was on his way up in Massachusetts. As he assumed the helm of the Patriots going into 1985, I wanted nothing more than for him to hire me as an assistant. I was talking with him regularly over the phone, but he wouldn't pop the question. I wondered, *Why won't he hire me?*

It was hard for a young, impulsive guy to understand someone as careful and deliberate as Raymond, who prayed about everything. As a matter of fact, he went to a cabin in New Hampshire where he fasted and prayed over every staff position. The upshot of his prayerfulness was that, as he said, "God told me to hire you."

I had been humbled—but not enough to be any less of a control freak. I told Raymond I wanted to coach both the quarterbacks and the receivers so that I could have my hands on the entire passing game. He went along with the idea and gave me a bright assistant named Harold Jackson to work with. There was no nominal offensive coordinator on that staff, and we made it work well.

I was back on the field, back in the fold; back on the road of ambition; back to hurrying along. And back to being under Raymond's watchful eye—as a coach and as a human soul.

The Super Bowl Shuffle

As we come to 1985, all of this sets up another classic NFL trivia question.

Every football fan remembers the 1985 Bears—a cultural phenomenon, really. *Saturday Night Live* featured a skit about their fans who picked "da Bearssss" to win any game, anytime, against any opponent, even if they fielded a team of "eleven mini-Ditkas." The players had a hit song and rap video called "The Super Bowl Shuffle." It was all over television before the Super Bowl was even played, and our children were dancing to it, to our chagrin. America really embraced that team. The Bears were made for media.

The Chicago Bears were coached by Mike Ditka and led by the legendary Walter Payton, the irrepressible Jim McMahon, the mammoth "Refrigerator" Perry, and quite possibly the most devastating defense ever unleashed on a gridiron, led by linebacker Mike Singletary.

Now for your trivia question: Who was da Bearssss' Super Bowl victim?

Good guess. That would be us, the '85 New England Patriots, coached by the rookie Head Coach Raymond Berry. What a comeback from the miseries of 1984, when I'd suffered through a three-win season. Now I was in the Super Bowl with a first-year head coach who was having the exact opposite experience I'd had the year before. I knew Raymond was a great man who was receiving the rewards of diligence and faith. I felt fortunate to be a part of something so rewarding after a year that was so discouraging.

Amazingly, we prevailed in three road games in the playoffs, culminating with a victory over Miami in a pouring rain. That one was a shocker. For one thing, the Dolphins were the only team that had beaten the Bears in the regular season. For another, the Patriots had lost to Miami eighteen consecutive times in the Orange Bowl, including a loss in game fifteen of 1985.

But we got it done, 31–14, and we were on our way to Super Bowl XX in New Orleans. We certainly were going to have our hands full on offense. Chicago ran what we call a "46 Defense" that was giving everyone fits that season. It meant blitzing five to eight players on every down, so an offense had trouble getting into rhythm. Finally, opposing coaches countered it with quick-timing passes and multiple-receiver formations, but it would take a couple of years for that to happen. In 1985 the Bears had the most bruising defensive attack going.

Chicago came in as a ten-point favorite. Since this was the twentieth Super Bowl, the MVPs from all the past games came in, and Bart Starr, Green Bay's MVP from Super Bowls I and II, was the honorary coin tosser. The atmosphere was as festive as I'd always heard it was.

We were ecstatic about the way the game began. Chicago's legendary Walter Payton quickly fumbled the ball on the Bears' 19. Tony Franklin hit a 36-yard field goal and we hit a 3–0 lead. We had reason to hope, even with the bad omen of losing our tight end, Lin Dawson, with a broken leg on the drive. The game was stopped, a stretcher was brought in, and Dawson was gone. Our excitement was also tempered by the fact that Tony Eason, our quarterback, had a high fever at game time. He started the game, but he wasn't 100 percent. Unfortunately, these two physical setbacks were more indicative of what was to follow than our field goal was. The Bears scored the next forty-four points.

Nothing we called on offense worked against Buddy Ryan's 46 Defense. The Bears had as many sacks as we did rushing yards— seven. I think that statistic says it all. We were up against one of the most celebrated NFL teams ever, and we were a "Cinderella" team that had overachieved just to get where we were. In short, we were in over our heads.

Our total yardage at halftime was -19, and what followed was a 21–0 third quarter for the Bears. Then the game's signature moment came late in that period when the Bears inserted William "Refrigerator" Perry, their massive defensive tackle, to score from one yard out and make the score 44–3. America loved it; the Patriots, not so much.

How does a coach handle such a blowout on international television? Hopefully he stays cool, he keeps calling plays, and he encourages his men to fight the good fight. Quitting isn't an option—least of all in a Super Bowl. We made it a small point of pride to stop Walter Payton from beating us with his running gifts. His longest gain was seven yards, and we held him to sixty-one without a touchdown. He had opportunities on the goal line, and Jim McMahon handed him the ball, but we swarmed number 34 and kept him from scoring.

We did finally get a touchdown early in the fourth quarter on a pass to Irving Fryar. But the rest of the game was typically Chicago-dominated. The one-sided defeat was painful, but we recognized the greatness that the Chicago Bears achieved that season. It was their year. Besides, getting by a lot of excellent teams to represent the AFC in the Super Bowl that season was itself an astonishing accomplishment for the New England Patriots.

Chalk Talk

As the off-season began, I found myself to be a hot commodity again. In the NFL, you can go from the penthouse to the outhouse and back again faster than a speeding elevator. I realized that it was more about the culture than about me. The NFL world is a turbulent place. The devastation of 1984 didn't mean I was a bad coach or person, and the redemption of 1985 didn't mean I was anything special. There are so many other dynamics at work: timing, the people around you, the teams around you, the plan of God, and your own wisdom and maturity.

I had a better understanding of that now. And I was eager to sit under the guidance of the Raymond Berrys and Tom Landrys of the world—father figures who had gone so much further than I in football and in faith. Even as my own stock improved, I knew I had much to learn.

That's why I was thrilled to have another opportunity to talk with Coach Landry. A few weeks after the Super Bowl, I was at the NFL Combine where college football's top players come to impress the scouts and make it to the next level. It's one of those times when the entire NFL family is together in one place. That year the combine was at the New Orleans Superdome, where the Patriots had just lost to the Bears in the Super Bowl. Gil Brandt, the Dallas general manager, approached me to talk about coming to Dallas. This made the third time the Cowboys had shown interest in me.

I'd only been with the Patriots for one season, but I was working on a one-year contract. That was by my own request. Back in 1978, Raymond Berry had advised me to work that way from year to year. That way, he said, you're flexible all the time. If the Lord says *go*, you can go. He may have been thinking of James 4:14: "How do you know what will happen tomorrow? For your life is like the morning fog— it's here a little while, then it's gone."

I was in a fog myself. I was on my way to talk to Tom Landry. Maybe the third time would be the charm.

Coach Landry greeted me cordially in his hotel room. I made the usual pleasantries—the honor of meeting him, his influence on me, and so on. After a few minutes he waved me to a blackboard and invited me to talk a few Xs and Os—the native language of coaches.

This was my moment to shine. I couldn't wait to show what I knew. He asked questions and I answered them—and then some. I talked rapidly, scribbled furiously, schemed and dreamed and testified. I could have talked all night.

Unfortunately, Coach Landry couldn't have listened to it. After three hours, he looked at his watch and said, "Well, Les, it's kind of late now." He stood, signaling the end of the meeting. He walked me to the door, offered his hand, and said, "I want to thank you for coming tonight." Then, as I walked out the door, he said, "Les, you're the most aggressive person I've ever met."

I said, "Thanks, Coach."

But as I turned and headed down the hotel corridor, I was beginning to feel that something wasn't right. I looked up and saw, through the oversized windows, the New Orleans Superdome where the Patriots had taken a beating so recently. It stood lit against a dark night sky. Suddenly I was hearing again Coach Landry's parting words.

"Les," I said to myself, "I don't think he meant them as a compliment."

Dallas and Dove Ranch

"The most aggressive person I've ever met . . ."

How aggressive must that be? A veteran NFL football coach has to have known some real predators. Is that how I came across? Is that what he got out of my chalk talk? I realized that Coach Landry had seen two sides of me: a fellow sitting in his living room, broken and humbled by a firing; and another fellow in front of a blackboard, talking fast and spouting answers—the most aggressive guy out there. I thought I knew which one impressed him least.

His subtle statement penetrated my heart. His words slipped deep inside me like seeds into fertile soil.

A few weeks later, with Raymond's permission, I flew to Dallas for a more official interview with Tex Schramm, the president of the Cowboys. It was all very secretive and hush-hush. Everyone knew that Coach Landry would be retiring before long, and he was looking for someone to bring in some fresh philosophy and maybe lay claim to succeeding him.

The organization virtually sneaked me into their new facility at Dove Ranch. Schramm told me that Coach Landry was interested in making some changes in his offense, liked my work, and what did I think?

I said that I had made the mistake of following a legend once before. I followed one up north, and if this thing worked out, I might well be following one down south. If so, I would request my contract to have one escape clause.

I had Schramm's attention. He said, "What's that?"

I said, "Well, Don Shula's going to retire sooner or later. I'd want permission to go to Miami and follow *his* legend."

Schramm laughed hard, clapped me on the back, and said, "You've got a great sense of humor."

It turned out that I wasn't the only candidate for the job. A young coach named Paul Hackett got the position after a strong recommendation from Bill Walsh, head coach of the San Francisco 49ers.

As far as working with Coach Landry was concerned, I figured three strikes meant I was out. But I knew that God has his timetable, and his plans are perfect. Still, I remember telling an interviewer that my two greatest disappointments were failing my physical to enter the U.S. Naval Academy and missing an opportunity to work with Tom Landry in Dallas. I had that much respect for him, and I often held him up to others as my model of wise leadership.

There's a story in the Bible in which a boy named Samuel, destined to be a prophet, hears his name called three times in the night. On each occasion he runs to his mentor, Eli, and asks, "Did you call me?" Each time Eli tells the boy he was mistaken. Finally, Eli takes Samuel aside and explains to him that God must be the one who is doing the calling.

In my case, a mentor called three times and I came running. But he never hired me. And I had to realize that even with Coach Landry's affection for me and my deep respect for him, the voice was coming from elsewhere. God was the one who was trying to get through to me. He wanted to become the father figure I was seeking. If I could have heard him clearly, I think he might have said that he had me right where he wanted: under the wing of Raymond Berry, who was something of an Old Testament prophet himself.

So that's where I stayed and coached, drawing a little closer each day to an inevitable showdown with the most dangerous enemy a man can face: himself.

Do You Have Any Peace?

Going to the Super Bowl after 1985 was a healing influence. I had stumbled, been humbled, and enjoyed a moment of grace. But it was going to take more distress for me to find out just where I was emotionally and spiritually.

The Patriots won the AFC East championship in 1986. Making the playoffs defines a successful season. In 1987 we missed the playoffs in the final game of the season. So we had gone from Super Bowl to playoffs to just missing the playoffs. We wanted to reverse the trend in 1988.

Once again, our fate came down to the final game. We had to play at Denver with our third-string quarterback because Tony Eason and Steve Grogan were both injured. Tom Ramsey stepped in and did a great job for us. He was a clutch player throughout the season, coming in so many times to lead us to victory. Unfortunately, the Broncos returned an interception for a late fourth-quarter touchdown, and we lost. Out of the playoffs again.

I rose from my seat in the press box, filled with anger, and stepped into the elevator. The team's owner was there. He saw that every cell of my being was filled with intensity, and he reached over and touched my forearm. "Coach," he said. "It's going to be all right."

"All right?" I snapped. "That's crazy! It's not going to be all right!"

That's not the best formula for addressing the guy who signs your paycheck. But somehow I wasn't fired—not yet, anyway.

But Raymond was watching.

Raymond knew me very well. He knew I was motivated, intense, driven. He knew that I would have done almost anything to be a head coach again. He knew I was on a mission to show the world that the Minnesota Vikings were wrong. He knew that I could be deceptive and manipulative, that I was always in competition with the other coaches, and that winning and success outweighed character and integrity on my scale.

A few weeks earlier, I had been walking rapidly down the hall on my way to the team meeting room on a Wednesday morning. It was my job to present the week's game plan. Raymond stopped me in the hallway and put his hand on my shoulder. He said, "Les, you're a Christian, aren't you?"

What an odd question at an odd time. I said, "Well, yeah, Raymond."

He studied me calmly for a moment and said, "Les, do you have any peace in your life?"

I could only reply, "Raymond, I've got a game plan to present." And I made my escape.

I tried to shut it all out and focus on Xs and Os. But the voices . . .

"Do you have any peace in your life?"

"You're the most aggressive person I've ever met."

Something inside me was churning. I knew that Raymond was right; that Tom Landry was right. Most of all, I knew that God was trying to get through—that my inner world was in complete turmoil, and the evidence was that I had no peace in my life. Everyone from the owner on down could see it.

It was shortly after that heartbreaking game against Denver, at the end of the 1988 season, that Raymond called me into his office. He said words I'll never forget:

"Les, the good Lord told me to hire you in 1985, and now he is telling me to fire you."

I felt as if I had been hit in the stomach. I hardly heard him as he said something about feeling that I had emotional problems and needed counseling. Raymond was marking the beginning of a new period for me—the worst period of my life. It was a season of brokenness.

I had intended to prove to the world that Les Steckel was a great coach. But here I was again, out of work, out of confidence, out of excuses. After the Vikings debacle, I could blame the situation, the management, whatever. Now it wasn't so easy to play that game. This had been a winning season for the Patriots. We had barely missed the playoffs. Yet I was fired again.

I was angry with Raymond, yet I knew he was a good man; he had a rock-solid integrity that I couldn't deny. What did he have that I didn't? I remembered running to his room the morning of the Super Bowl, chattering about the game. There was Raymond, on this day of all days, sitting in his bathrobe, reading his Bible. Here was Raymond, a first-year coach like I had been, but *peaceful.* He prayed while I pressed. Yet he was a first-year head coach in a Super Bowl. That was a difference I could understand.

I understood more than that, however. I knew he was right about the turmoil inside me; about my lack of peace. I knew that Coach Landry was right about my aggression. And for some reason, I thought of my father. I suddenly understood why Raymond was always asking about my father.

"Tell Me about Your Father"

Raymond had a way of asking the last question you expected. He'd say, "Tell me about your father. What was he like? Did he compliment you?"

I had no idea what my dad had to do with anything. I had a great dad. But I would begin to talk. I'd tell the "Pumper" stories.

Pumper was what my dad's buddies called him. He was a guy who was fighting all his life. He fought in World War II. He fought his way to a college education—the first in his family, an honor he embraced. He taught toughness, integrity, honesty, and a fierce determination to succeed. This was a guy who worked two jobs for thirty-eight years, and he wouldn't tolerate anyone in his family refusing to work hard. It was hard for me to get involved in sports over the summers, because I had to work two jobs like him.

When I was twelve, I said, "Dad, I want to play football."

He flatly refused.

I kept after him about it—I really wanted to play. Finally, he said I could go out for the team if I read Mark Twain's *Huckleberry Finn* and *Tom Sawyer* and passed his test on them. Dad was a high school math teacher, and education was a priority with him. But I couldn't figure out what those books had to do with football. I thought I could fake my way through the requirement, but sure enough, he gave me a test and I failed. Then I had to beg for a second chance and actually read both of those books. I passed the test the second time, but by then it was several weeks into the season, and there were kids sixteen years old on the junior high team. There were older, larger, and tougher kids who had failed a grade or two and stayed on the younger team.

I had come out to practice late, so I was the tackling dummy. It took drive to survive—that's what I was learning. After that seventh grade season, my dad didn't allow me to play football again until my senior year. I knew Dad wouldn't give me permission, so I went out and practiced with the team without it. Finally, it came time for the first game, and our coach reminded me I had never turned in a parental permission slip.

"C'mon, Coach," I said. "You know I can play."

"I can't let you into a game without that signature, Steckel. You know that."

My heart sank. My friend Denny Peters tossed me his car keys and said, "Go for it." I dashed home and clomped into the kitchen dressed in my cleats and shoulder pads. My mom and dad were sitting at the kitchen table reading the newspaper. "Dad," I said, pleading. "Please—sign this thing."

He looked up, took in the sight of me all dressed out, and went back to ignoring me. I just stood there and begged and bargained until he finally gave in.

I went on to have a great senior season, and my dad took credit for it by saying he had let a lion out of his cage. He was right. I was one angry young man.

Raymond Berry used to express curiosity over whether my dad ever complimented me. The honest answer is *never*. As a matter of fact, after I became an NFL coach, my dad once told my wife, "The reason Les is where he is today is because I never complimented him."

That was true. When I came home and proudly handed him my Golden Gloves boxing trophy, his only comment was, "George Daskalaskis could kick your butt." George was a local kid known as a tough fighter.

It seemed that the older I got, the more competitive I became—and the more likely I was to end up in a brawl. Raymond caused me to take a second look at those old days. He helped me see what was happening inside me. I was still trying to get that compliment that never came. I was searching for my dad's approval, whether it was in Raymond Berry or Tom Landry. I was searching for Dad in some new form—someone who embodied toughness and integrity but who would tell me that I was a good person doing a good job.

God used all of them as father figures, but he said things through them that I didn't want to hear; things I couldn't afford to ignore.

He used Tom Landry to say, *You're too aggressive.*

He used Raymond Berry to say, *You have no peace inside.*

And finally, there was the voice of the Father of all fathers, the Father of us all. And he was saying, *Come aside with me. We have work to do.*

Driven, Not Called

I came across a book that ultimately turned my world around. It was Gordon MacDonald's *Ordering Your Private World* (Nelson Books, 1984), and I came to a section in it that was like reading my life story. As a matter of fact, I wrote "Les Steckel's Biography" in the margin.

Dr. MacDonald wrote about two kinds of people: those who are *driven* to perform and those who are *called.* He absolutely nailed me when he described drivenness as:

- Gratified by accomplishment; having to achieve to feel good about himself.
- Preoccupied with the power: titles, office size, positions.
- Constantly pursuing larger opportunities; never satisfied.
- Disregarding integrity.

- Lacking in people skills.
- Highly competitive.
- Volcanically temperamental.
- Abnormally busy.

The book came about in the mid-eighties, around the time when I was coming to understand just how driven I was, just how little peace I felt, and just how much chaos and emptiness I had inside me. Finally, I had the label for it: I was *driven*. To be driven is to be enslaved, but to be called is to be liberated. If only I could discover what it meant to be called, I could live and perform from the over-flow of joy and fulfillment rather than the incessant demands of success and accomplishment, which are never satisfied.

And why was I driven? I was coming to realize during this tough time that it was all about gaining basic approval—the kind we need from a parent. I had been searching for fatherly affirmation in all the wrong places. When I didn't receive it at home, I began to search for it every-where else in the world, but particularly through strong male leader-ship figures—through Bud Grant, through Tom Landry, through Raymond Berry. These men and others have been great mentors, but I know now that no human being on earth can free me from that enslavement of performance or give me the perfect, unconditional love and affirmation that I need.

There is someone else, however—another Father entirely. My heav-enly Father is the only one who can give my soul what it truly needs.

How often I've seen it in others as the years have gone by: the search for Dad; the thirst for his approval. You find it in all the cir-cles of influence today—the hard-drivers, the achievers, those fixated on success at any price. Bud Grant once told me, "Les, you know why there's so much insecurity in this league? Because it's filled with inse-cure people."

He was exactly right. You'd think an NFL player making several million a year would be the most confident and secure person in the world. But many of them will tell you a different story once they begin to open up. Many of today's players and coaches either had no father or had one they could never please. I'm convinced that the father's approval, or the lack of it, is a central issue in every man's life. If we don't confront it effectively, what will the damages be to our future? If we can come to grips with it positively, how much happier and healthier are we bound to be?

The Extra Point

What about you? If I were there at your elbow, maybe I'd pull a Raymond on you—I'd say, "Tell me about your father. What did it take to earn his approval? Did he ever praise you? Encourage you?"

When I speak to men about this subject today, I can see the emotion in their eyes; their desire for me to change the subject. As I begin to deal candidly with this issue, many men in the audience simply can't or won't confront it. Some of them will even leave the room.

I was there once, believe me. And let me assure you, it's not just natural but good to want to please a parent. But sometimes we become caught up in an endless spiral of trying to earn something that won't come—perhaps from someone who loves us, is proud of us, and has no clue exactly how to express it so that the love becomes real and tangible to us.

We all need to feel loved, but before long we can begin to act out unmet needs in every part of our lives. And, my friends, doing so can cause great damage to your career, your family, and your very soul. You will find no peace.

So what can you do about it? It's very difficult to let go of the past. I can't tell you there's a quick formula or an easy process for overcoming the scars of yesterday. But I can invite you to do the following:

- *Come to grips with your past.* Think hard about the family that raised you, particularly your father. The past is too powerful; you can run, but you can't hide.

- *Call it what it is.* If you didn't feel approval, acknowledge that fact. If you have been angry, acknowledge that fact too. Realize the negative effect anger can have.

- *Forgive. Period.* Yes, I mean it. Give your family the total, unconditional grace and mercy that God has given you. Sure, they're guilty of being imperfect. Aren't we all? Sincerely forgive and move on.

- *Feel the love.* Whatever we lack, God fills it in. His love is perfect. Simply ask him to help you feel and heal.

6

Brokenness: Going Deep

TRIPS LEFT   114   LITE   Y   SPIKE - GO DEEP

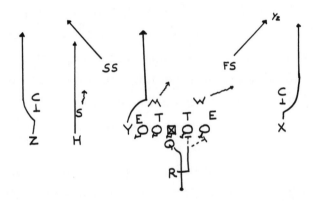

I was visiting an old friend named Dante Scarnecchia, and I always enjoyed being with him. But this day marked a bittersweet reunion. Dante was coaching with the Colts, and I was coaching with no one.

Indianapolis had come to Foxboro to play the Patriots, the latest team to let me go. The year was 1990, and I was like an alcoholic without his bottle, only my addiction was football.

I visited my buddy at the team hotel early that Sunday morning. He and I had jogged together regularly for four years when we coached together at New England.

"Dante, I want you to know something," I said. "If I ever . . . *ever* get another chance to coach, I'm going to do it differently."

"Les, don't be so hard on yourself," he replied. "You're a good coach, a great guy, and you'll be back in the league before you know it."

"Thanks, Dante, but it goes a little deeper than that. You see, Raymond was right to fire me. *I* would have fired me too. I deserved to be fired."

Dante nodded, but I could see that he was already putting on his game face. I knew the look and the feel of it. How I wished I was in his shoes. It didn't have to be for the Colts or the Patriots. Any team would have done.

It felt as if my life had come apart. There was a word for it: *brokenness.*

I had heard the word one time in my life. Back when the Vikings had just fired me, a woman in a church crowd had used the term. After I finished speaking, she came up to me and said, "I believe God removed you from that position to put you through brokenness."

Brokenness? What's that? I told the woman I had no idea what she was talking about. And I was being honest, for even after the Vikings fiasco, I still didn't get it.

Now, a few years later, I got it. I understood what brokenness was all about. Thirteen months is enough time to process a great deal of emotional truth.

Picture a Sunday in my life during that year of 1990—my year without football. We still had our home in Foxboro, just a mile from the stadium. Given the hill we were situated on, we could see the stadium from our front yard. We could hear the roar of the crowd.

On Sunday mornings, we would rise and go to Sunday school and church. That congregation was a mighty fortress for us during those months. I counted Gene Heacock, the pastor, as a close friend. Raymond Berry knew that. He had noticed the two of us working out together in the weight room. Raymond is a sensitive person, ministry-driven at all times. When the time came to cut me loose, he picked up the phone and called Gene. He clued the pastor in and encouraged him to reach out to an aching soul.

So we never missed church. Then, on a September Sunday afternoon, I would crank up the lawn mower. Why would I do this on Sunday? Maybe I was punishing myself. I'd push the machine up and down slopes of our front yard, with that packed stadium in the corner of my eye. I knew I could see the press box if I turned and looked. Someone else was calling the plays there, doing the thing I loved. And I could hear the crowd thundering their approval and almost feel the electricity.

Then I would cut off the lawnmower in the middle of the task. I'd run up our driveway and dash through the garage into the house. I would pick up speed—pass the study and hit the stairway, taking two steps at a time on my way to the bedroom. I would pull the door shut behind me, push in the lock button, and fall on my knees at the bed, weeping bitterly.

Broken.

I wish I could have found that wise woman in Minnesota and told her that yes, now she and I were speaking the same language.

I remember waiting for the phone to ring. Coaches live and die by the telephone. It rings at the best times, conveying job offers, pay raises, chats with coaching pals or players who have made good and want to call and say thanks. That ring can also rock your world—bring the news that you have no job. The telephone giveth; the telephone taketh away.

But worst of all is when the telephone is silent. During this period, nobody called. There were no offers, no gossip, nothing but silence from the NFL community. I told Chris that maybe this was it. Maybe the door marked Football was closed and my coaching days were over. I began looking in the direction of the Marine Reserves, in the direction of other careers, and I contemplated what it would be like to start my life all over again.

I was feeling the heat. I had come to the furnace of life, the place where steel is refined and the future is defined. I was going to learn something about myself, and I was going to come out of it stronger and wiser.

But the hard thing about refining fire is that first, you have to survive the heat.

An Inside Job

Before we move on, let's rewind the tape one year—back to the end of the 1988 season when I lost my job with the New England Patriots, just before Christmas. The first thing I did was take Raymond Berry's advice. He had said I needed counseling. Those words were painful, but I knew he was right. So I called a sports psychologist who had consulted with the Patriots since 1985.

Joe Cautella was a wise and demanding counselor. He had a way of helping me confront drives and motives I had never been willing to face. The first time we met was over lunch. He asked a lot of questions, and I seemed to answer every one of them the same way: "Not me. Not me. Not me." I was playing "prevent defense" all the way. "I don't do that," I said. "I don't do this; that's not me." I was in strict denial. I was backpedaling like a defensive back. Sometimes the truth is so painful, we let it sink in only very slowly.

On the way home from our lunch together, I thought, *Les, were you listening to yourself?* I wanted to get some answers, and I wanted to put my problems behind me and get back to a sideline and a clipboard somewhere. But I was just beginning to realize how much work I had to do and how much it was going to hurt. This wasn't something you could neatly wrap up at a weekend retreat.

Coach Bill McCartney once told me, "Les, I've never seen anyone who can internalize things more than you can." Well, now it was time to go inside and externalize them. It was like taking an elevator ride to the depths of my soul and finding all the toxic stuff that had accumulated since childhood. During the next thirteen months, I broke a lot of shovels cleaning that furnace. The truth is, I'm still working at it after all these years, with the difference being that I know what's inside me, and I'm willing to do the maintenance.

I had always said that my priorities were *faith, family,* and *football*— in that order. But I learned that the real list was *me, myself,* and *I.* I was willing to sacrifice anything and anyone on the altar of my hungry ambition. Having been raised under the banner of "You can't do anything right," I was on a mission now to prove that I could do everything better than anybody else. And that agenda was leaving a path of destruction in my wake, the greatest victim being yours truly.

In three or four sessions of counseling, it all came flooding out. On the one hand, the truth hurt. But on the other hand, I was able to face it on football terms. I attacked my brokenness as if I were showing up in August for preseason drills. The difference was that I was disciplining my spirit instead of my body. I worked at it. I took notes. I focused.

Most of all, I tried to break myself of the illusion that I was the center of the universe. "I am a child of God," I said to myself. "He put me on this planet, and now he's breaking me like a wild stallion standing on its hooves, kicking and braying. If I'm ever going to run the race the way he designed me, then I have to let him break me and retrain me and yield to his reins."

Slowly but surely, God led me along. Painfully but obediently, I followed. I felt that if ever I was given another chance, I could run with fresh legs and a new spirit. The question was whether God still had races for me to run.

What Can Brown Do for You?

The Patriots had fired me after the 1988 season. One day shortly afterward, my brother, Dave, called to tell me about a coaching opportunity he had heard about. Despite an eleven-year age difference, Dave and I have always shared a special bond that comes from our Marine Corps and college coaching experiences. Dave has had a great career in coaching college football.

"Les," he said, "Brown University is looking for an offensive coordinator."

Brown University? Was he talking about the Ivy League? I reacted immediately with the old pride and ambition. I had been an NFL head coach. I had been to a Super Bowl. Even when I coached in the college ranks, it had been with powerful Colorado. What would my old coaching friends think about my taking a job with a team that sat at the bottom of the college computer rankings, just one above Columbia?

This job would be close enough that I wouldn't have to move my family. My kids were settled into their schools. We loved our church and our community. The lure of coaching had lost none of its strength. I picked up the phone.

John Rosenberg was the head coach at Brown. I went to three formal interviews, and finally John leaned back in his chair and sighed. He looked at me closely and said, "Les, we didn't win a single game last year. I'm just telling you that we could get fired at the end of the season."

"So what else is new?" I replied, and we laughed. Such is the coaching life.

Brown was a little broken at this point, but so was I. I cared deeply about the kids, and I hear from some of them to this day. Hungry for the coaching experience, I poured myself into that new job. During August, Chris took off with the kids to spend time in California with her parents. I slept on a lawn chair in my office rather than drive back to Foxboro. Though it was only a half-hour commute from Providence, Rhode Island, I was putting in late hours to build a really special offense—something to lift the spirits of a group of kids who hadn't known victory in a long time.

Coach Rosenberg had warned me that as soon as the depth chart went up at the end of two-a-days, there would be a mass exodus. Kids would quit because of the prospect of not making the two-deep roster (first and second strings). The classroom was tough enough at Brown; why should these kids hang around if they stood no chance of seeing the field? We were going to lose a lot of players.

Not on my watch, I thought and put my mind to work. A couple of years earlier, I might not have been so creative. But the lesson I was learning was, *It's not about me.* It was about these outstanding student-athletes who wanted to get onto the field—a feeling I could well remember.

So we called a meeting. I told the kids, "Here's the deal, and here's my word. Stay on this team, and you will play in every home game you dress out for and every road game if you make the travel squad."

The kids looked at each other as if I were claiming the moon was made of green cheese. But I went on to lay out exactly how we would get it done: twenty-three different personnel groupings; a role for every young man who wanted to stick around.

The plan worked well. The offense had new life, new zip, and there was a buzz among the alumni. The team was still losing games, often by a 35–33 type of score. But we were putting points on the board and playing more jersey numbers than ever.

By the end of the season, it became clear that, just as John had foretold, he was going to be fired. What he hadn't expected was that there would be a parallel movement to make me the head coach. Out in the parking lot after a game, I told the athletic director not to even think about it. He wanted to know why not.

I said, "Because John is a fine coach, and he's giving it his best. And because I don't want to give the appearance of an ex-NFL coach waiting in the wings, plotting to get his job." Because it wasn't about me, I could think about John, who deserved better treatment.

It wasn't until the end of the season that John was fired, along with the rest of the staff. In no time, the alumni began courting me to take his place. But I knew that wasn't where I was supposed to be. At one point I was asked, "If you take this head coaching job, how do we know you won't jump to the NFL after a year?"

"You don't," I said. "That very thing could happen." Because it wasn't about me, I could be honest rather than deceptive. It felt good.

It was becoming clear I needed to move on. But it was a decision that put me out of work for the time being. Ultimately it would mean a year out of football, a year to do nothing but keep working on fixing my brokenness. And every day, the absence of a coaching position seemed to take on additional weight and pain.

Reaching Bottom

After finishing the season at Brown, I was officially unemployed. I had never imagined I would stand in that line with the rest of the down-and-outers, waiting to pick up my check from the government. Another coach once told me, "I would never accept an unemployment check. I have too much pride in myself."

Not me. I wanted to provide for my family. Foxboro is a small town, and folks recognized me in the check line.

"Hi, Coach."

"You too, Coach?"

A nice woman behind a desk at the unemployment office felt my embarrassment and told me I could come in and quietly pick up my check without waiting in the public line. I was grateful and humbled.

I also used this time to go back on active duty with the Marine Reserves. Doing so helped us make our mortgage payment. But I knew what was happening. You have to reach the bottom before you can turn around and head for the top. You have to die before you can be reborn. Every day I asked God to help me through it, to humble me, to destroy any pride, to help me learn what it meant to be helpless and totally dependent on him for my future. Depending on my own ambition certainly hadn't worked.

But the hardest part was going "cold turkey" from coaching. One day the full brunt of my loss hit me square in the face. I was on reserve duty in California, and I sat down and turned on the television. There on the screen were the Raiders. I turned up the volume.

After one play, I said, "I'm really not there." The whole NFL universe was proceeding as if I'd never been a part of it. It was like watching the world after your own death. After a second play, I thought, *I can't take this*. I clicked off the power and sat for a while, just staring into space and an empty future.

August, September. It was really happening. The 1990 football season was here, and the phone had never rung. Finally, I told Chris, "If I don't coach again, I'll go crazy." And I couldn't believe my own actions when I picked up the phone, called Foxboro High School, and asked for the football coach. I introduced myself and explained that it was my first year out of coaching. I expressed a desire to help with the high school players, strictly on a volunteer basis.

He said, "You're kidding."

I said, "Not at all. It's my first year out, and I just want to offer my assistance. No salary required."

He said, "That's amazing. Well, let me introduce you to the other coaches." So I visited the school, we had a great talk, and I met the other guys. The coach told me he'd be in touch.

But weeks passed, and the phone didn't ring.

Finally, I called back, and the coach couldn't come to the phone. I left a message that wasn't returned. When I finally managed to get his attention, he sheepishly told me it wasn't going to happen. "We don't need your help," he said.

So that was that. Thanks, God—the unemployment line didn't

faze me, but now I think I'm beginning to learn what this humility thing is all about. Five years ago, I was coaching in a Super Bowl. Now I couldn't get my call returned from the local high school coach.

So I stubbornly pushed forward. I dared to get on with my life—a life, it appeared, free of football. I dared to mow my lawn in full view of the stadium and found out I couldn't do it. I couldn't even watch football on television. It was just too painful. Again and again I ended up on my knees in the bedroom, struggling with the turmoil inside me.

There was still a lot of shoveling to do down in that furnace.

Where to Now?

"Chris," I said quietly, "I may never coach again. That's just the reality of it—that chapter of our life may be finished. It's time for us to decide where to go and what to do. Should we stay here in New England? Is there a better place to raise our kids? A better place for me to find a job that isn't sports-related? Where do we put down our roots and start again?"

I was quite serious. It was late October and time to be realistic. "In fact," I continued, "take a couple of hours to think and pray on it, Prep. Go somewhere and get a cup of coffee. I'll watch the kids."

Chris said, "Great, I'm out of here," and proceeded to a little café to do some tall thinking. When she returned, I asked her what she had decided.

"Charlotte," she said.

"Who?"

"Charlotte, North Carolina."

"Prep, are you serious? Why?"

My wife had a simple answer: *expansion team.* Charlotte was soon going to join the NFL family. My wife, being the person she is, was thinking only of what she thought would make me happy. She was willing to go anywhere and live any life, but she understood that I needed to coach.

I said, "That's an answer for me, not for you. I want to know where *you* would be happiest."

And we bantered back and forth and came to one of those moments in which nobody wanted to say what they were thinking first. When that happens, we have a little ritual where we count to three and, at the exact same time, blurt out our answers. So we did that: "One . . . two . . . three . . .

"*Boulder.*" Two voices in perfect unison. Two hearts beating as one. Boulder, Colorado.

Boulder was where it had all started for us. It was our first married home; my first coaching job; a beautiful city with beautiful memories. Now we had a young family, and Boulder could only be that much better.

We couldn't just load up the station wagon and drive to Colorado, of course. We had no plan, no job waiting, no home there. Just the same, I picked up the telephone—the coach's best friend and worst enemy. I started making calls in Boulder and Denver. The first man I called was an old friend named John White. He and his wife, Barbara, are still among our dearest friends. I asked him to be on the lookout for openings and opportunities of any kind. Any available job was on the table. Coaching was out anyway, because the hunting season for NFL coaching jobs is New Year's to March 1. We just wanted to come to Boulder.

A little more than a month passed. Late in November, John White called. He said, "Les, I really believe God is telling me that you need to meet with Bill McCartney. Do you know Bill?"

I certainly did know the head coach of the Colorado Buffaloes. We had met at an FCA conference back in 1978. But what an odd thing for John to say—that he was taking counsel from God himself. I said, "Well, okay. Thanks." And I hung up.

Several hours later the phone rang again. John White. "Les, I took the liberty to make contact with Coach McCartney. He's out of the office, but it turns out he'll be in New York City on December 1."

"John, I appreciate it, but that's only a couple of days away."

"It sure is. You need to get to NYC and see him."

"John, this isn't exactly how . . ."

"I'm dead serious. I'm telling you. Go and see Coach McCartney."

My friend was so intent on this idea that I had to respect it. So I called Mac's office out in Colorado and left a message. He recognized the name and called me right back. "Les," said Bill McCartney, "I'm on my way to New York City for an awards banquet."

"So I'm told. May I come down there and see you?"

Mac replied, "Sure, I'd like that."

Late on a Thursday night, I got up, left our home Bible study group early, and drove to New York City. I was in the Big Apple at midnight, in bed by one thirty, and up again at five to shower and shave for my get-together with Bill.

Mac and I strolled through Central Park, sharing our lives and catching up with coaching stuff. We didn't know each other very well, and there was nothing remarkable about our conversation. No real sparks were produced. As we turned back to the hotel, I laid my cards on the table. "Bill, let me tell you what's on my heart. I'd love to move my family back to Colorado. I have no idea whether there's an opening on your staff. But I love Boulder, I love football, and I'd love to work for you."

Mac said, "That's terrific. I really appreciate it." Then he let me down gently. He told me that if there were an opening (and there didn't seem to be one), he already had another man in mind—someone he had wanted on his staff for a while. But he promised to keep me in mind.

Well, maybe John White had missed something. *Maybe it wasn't God after all,* I thought. At least Mac and I had enjoyed a good walk and gotten to know each other better.

A Christmas Gift

Meanwhile, I was in touch with the World Football League. Mike Lynn, who had been the general manager of the Vikings, was the president of the WFL and had been promising to make me a head coach. To make a long story short, that prospect came up empty too—right after the meeting with Coach McCartney.

A tough year was coming to a fittingly cold ending. I had been rejected at every level of football above Pop Warner. I had stood in unemployment lines. I was one shell-shocked marine and one humble former NFL coach. The only thing I knew was that when the world was disappointing, God was faithful. When people were merciless, God's love was everlasting, overflowing. One Saturday afternoon after my reserve duty, I was driving home in our big blue van. I screamed out, "I'm yours—all of me!" I recommitted myself wholly to his guidance. I was broken but clear-eyed. I knew my only hope was in him.

On Christmas Eve, I was calling out to our kids to climb into the van. We were running late for the candlelight service at church. As I was walking down the stairs, I was reflecting on my third straight Christmas of unemployment. I'd been fired after the 1988 season, then lost the Brown job after the 1989 season. By Christmas of 1990, my spirits were at their lowest. Yet my prayer life had never been better. I was reading the Bible every day and trying to let my wife and kids see Christ in me, even through my brokenness. At Christmastime, I wanted my family to be able to look into my eyes and know that the Spirit of the living God lived inside me. I was holding back tears. This was the third Christmas in a row that I was without a job. I was down, very down. As I helped Chris with her coat and began getting into my own, the phone rang.

When the phone rings at this time of year, a coach stops and stares for a second. He thinks about what sharp new turn the path of his life may take. Promotion or firing? Time freezes, and it takes a deliberate effort to reach for the ringing receiver.

But now was different, I told myself. No one could fire a jobless guy. Especially one who had been rejected by the local high school team.

How long did we let the phone ring? *How bad can it be?* I thought. And I picked up the receiver. "Hello?"

"Les, this is Bill McCartney. I'm calling from Miami. I'm sure you know we're getting ready to play Notre Dame in one week for the national championship at the Orange Bowl."

My throat went very dry.

Mac continued, "It may sound strange, Les, but this very moment, God put it on my heart to call you and offer you a job at the University of Colorado. I don't know what that job is. I don't know what I can pay you. All I know is I had a powerful impression to call you on the phone and offer you a job. Sorry I can't talk any longer, but I'm late to a staff meeting. May I call you back Tuesday?"

I stammered a yes. There was a click and the dial tone returned.

Chris said, "What?"

I repeated the conversation in awe. With our eyes wide, Chris and I climbed into the van. Within minutes, we were pulling up to the church. The glass windows were shining brilliantly in the wintry evening sky. Candles twinkled like stars over Bethlehem. The moment was serene and beautiful and filled with Christmas peace and goodwill to all men, even brokenhearted football coaches. Chris and I just wanted to sit in the car and soak it in.

"Kids," I said, "run in and save us a pew."

We sat silently for a moment, thinking of the mystery, power, and abounding love of God. Finally I turned to Chris and said, "Well, Prep—what do you think?"

In a quiet voice, my best friend replied, "I think we need to go back to Boulder where we started eighteen years ago. And I think that this time, we do it his way."

In the new year, we headed out to Boulder to make that fresh start. After a year in the wilderness, a year in the furnace, a year of rejection and humility, God had restored our joy on Christmas Eve. I was offered a job with the NCAA national champions in the very city God had set in both of our hearts; a second chapter to begin in the very place where the first one had commenced. There's no moment like the one when you climb out of the furnace, refined and stronger, and feel the cool air of normality again.

A friendly graduate assistant picked me up at the airport and drove me to the Colorado Buffaloes' offices. And he led me to the new place set aside for me. There before me was the same office, the same desk, and the same chair in which my career had begun.

Lord, I get the message.

This time, your way.

The Extra Point

Let me share with you the mental image I've always carried about this experience. This is how I explain it: I was in the far left lane, moving at one hundred miles per hour, when God slammed on the brakes of my life. I skidded to the shoulder of the road, just short of going over the cliff, and caught my breath from the sudden shock.

I began to look into the rearview mirror. I reviewed my past to see what had brought me here, how I had picked up so much speed, and why I had been careening out of control. I needed to adjust the mirrors on each side to expose my blind spots. I had many, and I still have a few. But if God hadn't intervened, where would I be today? I'd rather not even think about it.

If you think this was a difficult chapter to read, you should have felt how hard it was to live.

Then again, I think you're smarter than I was years ago, when I didn't understand the meaning of the word *brokenness*. I have an idea you may have built up a little too much speed yourself at one time or another.

Brokenness is not an experience God reserves for coaches. It's such a powerful idea, such an effective tool for his purposes, that he uses it over and over again—for accountants, teachers, sales representatives, CEOs, craftsmen, homemakers, everyone.

You see, God designed this world and this life very carefully. When we do it his way, the world turns properly, things work well, and people are content and successful. When we grab the wheel and put the pedal to the floor, we crash into the powerful walls he built for our own protection. He knew that life works best when we live it unselfishly. He knew that life takes on beauty, peace, and resonance when it's not all about me.

But we're stubborn people, and we insist on opening up that engine and seeing just how fast it can fly. When that happens, it's not as if God watches dispassionately as we hit the skid. His plan is perfect; his love unfailing. He gently reaches into our lives to put things right, painful as it might be. Like that broken stallion, we have greater races to run—more swiftly, more wisely, for the majesty of his glory instead of the folly of our ambition.

One more way of saying it: the road to the crown travels by way of the cross. As we say in football: no pain, no gain. My favorite Bible verse is Luke 9:23. In it Jesus says that if you want to follow him, you must deny yourself, take up your cross daily, and follow him. He goes on to say that if we cling to the wreckage of the old life, we will lose it all, but if we let go, we will gain a new life.

Do you have the courage to pull to the side of the road and examine your life?

If you knew that your life could be everything you've dreamed, would you be willing to undergo your own time of brokenness in order to get there?

And finally, this question: Are you spiritually sensitive enough that if this experience comes to your life, you will recognize it for what it is? Will you know that failure is not final, that God can use every ounce of your pain to build something new and hopeful, and that your defeat can be turned to victory?

Brokenness is something no one wants but everyone needs. Only when we've become helpless can we understand how powerful God's hands are, how capable he is of fixing and restoring broken lives, and just how much more incredible life is going to be when we're on our feet once again—this time doing things his way.

7

Team Player

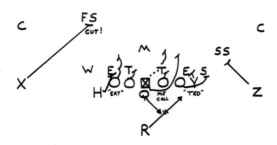

Chris walked to the mailbox on a chilly day in January 1991. Her thoughts wandered comfortably toward the future, as they so often did. I was in New Orleans recruiting for the Colorado Buffaloes. Chris looked forward to hearing from me that evening.

Life was good—finally. The Christmas Eve phone call from Bill McCartney had marked the end of a miserable interlude in our lives. Chris had seen me off to the Rockies to get our new life started—and to do it God's way this time. As usual, the plan was for me to hop on a plane and hit the ground running in my new job, while Chris stayed back to wind up old business—put the house on the market, prepare the kids for a move, wrap up all East Coast business.

Chris scanned the junk mail, magazines, and flyers without much interest. Then she saw the official-looking envelope and caught her breath. No! This was unthinkable—impossible! As she read the contents, her throat tightened and her heart began to race. She asked herself what in the world God had in mind.

For me, Colorado was an odd mixture of past memories and future hope. My first day back on campus, I stepped into the basketball coliseum. Years earlier, during my first sojourn on this campus, I'd had something to do with building this arena. NCAA regulations had come through, limiting the sizes of coaching staffs. Lacking seniority, I was the odd man out; I was asked to downgrade to a part-time coaching role. The rest of my job consisted of raising funds for a new basketball arena that would eventually be completed after I had moved on.

Now I saw the finished product. I wanted the new Les to turn out as impressively as the new arena had. I was under construction, after all. I was all about being more expansive, like this building; about having more room in my life for people.

In January 1990 I had taken a walk with Bill Curry at the annual coaches' convention in San Francisco. Bill was taking on the head coaching job at the University of Kentucky, and he was talking to me about joining his staff. As we strolled along near Fisherman's Wharf, Bill was up front with me. He said he had studied my résumé. He had talked to some of the other coaches on the New England staff. "Les, your credentials are impeccable," he said. "You've had success at every level. You've got the talent. But they tell me that your stumbling block is relationships. They say you have a hard time working with the other guys on the staff."

Not surprisingly, I wasn't seriously considered for that job. But I was determined to eliminate that stumbling block once and for all. Therefore, I arrived in Boulder with two serious goals:

- One, to devote myself to building relationships; to make people skills a strength instead of a weakness.
- Two, to live out Philippians 2:14: "In everything you do, stay away from complaining and arguing."

Unfortunately, I'd come to grips with the fact that I was a complainer. Chris said that it was the only negative part of my job that came home with me—constantly finding fault and harping on how I could do it better. It was all part of the *driven* Les Steckel.

It was time to drive out the drivenness. It was time to focus on people, particularly in the listening category.

It was no matter of false humility. I was here to learn a brand new offense I knew nothing about: the wishbone, a ground-oriented option attack. I intended to zip my lip, learn from the other coaches, and get to know everyone I could, right down to the maintenance people who emptied the wastebaskets. For the first time, I began to invest my time in getting to know graduate assistants, sports information directors, secretaries. And I was loving every minute of it.

At the same time, a great difference between the college and pro games is the emphasis on recruiting. The travel and the attention to eighteen-year-olds would challenge me to grow as a people person. A school like Colorado recruits nationally, so I was flying all over the place. Pretty soon I was down on the Louisiana bayou, heading for New Orleans to look up a talented kid by the name of Kordell Stewart. He was the top-rated wishbone quarterback in America, so he was a "must-sign" for one of the few wishbone offenses around. Kordell and I sat in a car during a heavy rainstorm and talked football for hours, hitting it off beautifully.

I was on top of the world when I called home to share my new excitement about recruiting with Chris. She is the kind of person who is always up, always steady. But there was something in her voice this time that quickly brought me back down to earth.

Yes, this was January 1991, and the Desert Storm invasion force was being assembled. I was still in the Marine Reserves, and Chris had opened my activation notice that very day.

Full Bird

Chris was upset about this sudden twist, just when things were going so well. "You're not going, are you, Les?" she asked. "You can't. You went to Vietnam—don't they know you've given your time?"

"I don't know, Prep. I just don't know," I said. "If they call me, it's my duty to go. But I'll see what I can find out."

Just when you think you know all the answers, they change the questions. Between being fired at Brown and hired at Colorado, I had endured thirteen months of misery. Now things were back on track. Never had God's workings seemed so visible, so compassionate, and so providential as when Bill McCartney called on Christmas Eve. There was even the Boulder angle—the very city Chris and I had named as our dream home.

Yet I must have already sensed something was up. I hadn't allowed Chris to sell the house in New England. For some reason I had felt that God was restraining me from pulling the trigger on that sale. Sure enough, now there was reason to believe we weren't moving to Boulder after all.

I called the marine headquarters in Washington, D.C., and asked whether my assignment was definite. "Orders are orders," said the officer.

All I could do was focus on my job and let the future take care of itself. I didn't tell Mac or anyone else what was up—I wanted to wait until my fate was official. But was I once more building something in Boulder that I would never see to fruition?

It was mid-January and I was due to report in about two weeks. Reserves have to be ready to get their houses in order quickly. I flew from New Orleans to Boston with a stopover in Newark. I decided to touch base with a very dear friend, Mike Sweatman. We had been through Kansas University and marine training together, and both of us had gone into coaching. He now had a great position on the staff of Bill Parcells with the New York Giants. In terms of military rank, Mike was a lieutenant colonel; I was what was called a "full bird colonel," the "bird" referring to the eagle on the insignia.

"Sweat," I said, "I got my job in Boulder, then I got my orders for Kuwait! Can you believe it?"

"No kidding!" Mike replied. He knew me well, and he understood the position I was in. I loved my country, my family, and my career. After a moment Mike said, "Know what, Les? America doesn't need you over there in the desert. I'm a body just like you, and it might as well be me over there. I'm going to give you my Social Security number so you can tell them to take me in your place."

"Sweat," I said incredulously. "Knock it off!"

"I'm as serious as I can be, Les." And the tone of his voice confirmed it.

"Sweat, I'm touched. Moved. But give me a break! Do you think I could let someone do my fighting for me?"

"Les, you've been out of work for thirteen months. They need you more in Boulder than in the Middle East. Got a pen? My Social Security number is—"

"Save it, Sweat."

"I'm giving it to you. Write it."

That's the kind of man Mike Sweatman is. Whether or not the Marine Corps would have considered his proposition didn't matter to me. It was no empty gesture—he was willing to place himself in harm's way for a friend. He exemplified the words of Jesus: "Greater love has no one than this, that he lay down his life for his friends" (John 15:13 NIV). Sweat is one of the humblest and most unselfish people I've ever known. He was Honor Man (top-ranked marine) when he graduated from Officers Candidate School, and then, twenty-six weeks later, he graduated as top man again at The Basics School. Mike was a marine's marine. He saw Desert Storm as his moment to serve his country and even his friend.

But I knew this was my responsibility. So back home, Chris and I nervously awaited word of my final status—one more time of waiting for the phone to ring. Finally, the marines called. An officer said, "This is in regard to Desert Storm. We have one question prior to issuing your orders."

I said, "Go ahead."

"Sir, are you a lieutenant colonel or a full bird colonel?"

"I'm an O6 full bird colonel," I answered.

The officer paused for a minute, then asked me to verify what I'd just told him. "Sir, you're a full bird colonel?"

"Yes, that's correct."

"Your orders have been canceled," said the officer. "We're not calling up full bird colonels. Our computer had you down as a lieutenant colonel, which would have required us to call you. Thank you, sir." And just like that, he hung up.

All that worrying over a computer error. Do you think I felt more gratitude than ever for God's plan to send me to Boulder? You'd better believe it. I had been within a few minutes of throwing my essentials into a duffle bag, kissing my wife and kids good-bye, and shipping out for the uttermost parts of the earth. Thousands of miles from American football.

Sometimes we just need a crisis to make all our life factors fall into place for us. At that moment, I had never been more grateful for the privilege of simply going to work, pursuing my calling, and providing for the family I loved.

Quick to Hear, Slow to Speak

These thoughts were in my heart as I cruised through the clouds on my flight back to Colorado. It was time for National Signing Day and hauling in a fresh batch of recruits, including Kordell Stewart from Louisiana, destined for NFL superstardom. It was also time for the staff to begin meeting and putting the offense together. Gary Barnett had just ascended to the position of offensive coordinator, with the national championship as his first game—an auspicious start.

So I was all about learning the wishbone and the triple option. The wishbone is a ground-oriented offensive attack that gives the quarterback three options: to run it himself, to hand the ball to the fullback on an up-the-middle dive, or to pitch the ball to the trailing back. I was eager to sit back and listen, soak in the plans and the people, and to establish a new and humbler approach on Bill McCartney's staff.

But one day a young graduate assistant named Scott Wachenheim spoke up. Scott had played four years at the Air Force Academy and was just getting into coaching. He was also a new Christian from a Jewish background, and he and I were on our way to becoming good friends. Scott is now the offensive coordinator at Liberty University.

One day while we were jogging after practice, as we did often, Scott suddenly blurted out, "Coach, we're dying to hear you talk."

I said, "About what, Scott?"

He said, "You've been a head coach in the NFL; a coordinator; you've been to a Super Bowl. Everybody talks about you after the meetings, saying they want to hear from you. Say something!"

I laughed and explained that I was here to learn all that I could from Gary and the rest of the staff.

"Talk about the passing game," he insisted. "Talk about *something!*"

But I wasn't interested in impressing people or claiming a turf. I was learning to be subservient to the team concept, and the staff was my team.

Months later, at the end of the season, Gary Barnett would be hired as head coach at Northwestern. He invited me to go there with him, and I knew Gary was a bright guy who was destined for success. But I was focused on the work in front of me—the work of learning to be a servant. I wasn't looking for a move.

Not that I didn't feel the growing pains. I believe God knew that putting me into this wishbone system was a good way of humbling me. Having become an NFL guy, I knew about pro sets and passing attacks. It's amazing I was even on this staff.

So it's not surprising that when we got into planning the offense, I had no input. What did I have to offer about the intricacies of running the option? Just the same, I struggled with impatience. I knew I had all my experience and all my creativity, and I had to keep it to myself.

I let my frustration build up inside until I lit into freshman Christian Fauria one day at practice. He was a top-notch tight end I had dubbed Rocky after the film character. He had that same persevering toughness to him. But on this day he wasn't locking the ball away. That was a simple fundamental that applied even to the wishbone, so it was something I could cling to; something I could harp on.

Normally, if a player mishandled the ball, I would say, "Come on, that's not the way to protect the football. Let's carry the ball correctly." But this time I went ballistic on Christian. I went overboard, berating him and humiliating him in front of everybody.

As the practice ended, I knew I had made a big mistake. This was exactly the kind of thing I was trying to put in my past—the driven side, resentful and negative and temperamental. I thought about what I should do as the players showered and headed for training table for dinner. After that, they'd be going their separate ways. But I headed off the receivers in the locker room and said, "Meeting room, right after your shower."

All fifteen kids came, wondering what I was going to say. "Guys," I began, "did you all hear what I did to Rocky on the field today? I embarrassed him out there. Not because he did anything to deserve it, but because I was *mad.* I was feeling frustrated at the moment, but it had nothing to do with you, Christian. So, guys, I took it all out on Rocky. Well, that was completely wrong, and I'm the one who is embarrassed now. I asked you all to come here so I can ask his forgiveness in front of everybody, just like I called him out in front of everybody. And I want all you guys to understand something. We are a *team,* and we're here to support one another. I'm here as your coach to serve you. Rocky, I want to ask your forgiveness."

He said, "Yeah, Coach. Sure, I forgive you. But you didn't have to do this."

I dismissed everybody and was alone with my thoughts. I made a commitment that I was going to live up to what I had just said. I was there to serve those kids.

Stepping Up

One day, during staff meeting, Bill McCartney told us a young man from Detroit would have to be kicked off the team. "Michael Westbrook is still missing classes and workouts," he said. "I've had enough of that. It's time for him to go. Does anyone have any comment?" The room was silent. This is something that happens in every college football program. We have kids from rough backgrounds who struggle with social behavior.

At the end of the meeting, Bob Simmons, another future head coach on our staff, came over and asked me if I knew who this troublesome kid was. Being new, I didn't.

Bob said, "You need to talk to him."

I said, "What? Why me?"

"Because I've been watching you," said Bob. "I see how you connect with kids, Les. I think Michael needs a second chance, and it seems to me that you're the guy who can help him."

I wasn't sure what I could do, but I walked upstairs and asked the secretary to get Michael Westbrook up to my office.

A few hours later he walked in. All I could think was, *Wow.* He was an impressive specimen of an athlete at six feet three, 215 pounds, *sculpted* more than built. This was definitely what God had in mind when he created the football player. His arms and shoulders were massive, and so was the chip that rested on them. Poor attitude just dripped from his body language.

I looked up at this athlete and said, "Michael, you and I are strangers. You don't know me, and I don't know you. People say you have huge potential on the football field, but it's about to become a moot point. Word is that Coach McCartney is going to call you into his office and dismiss you from the team."

A little of the attitude dissolved. My statement came as a total shock to him. "What?" he asked.

I said, "Michael, I've got one question for you. Would you be willing to work with me and take one final shot at hanging on here?"

Michael said, "I can't go back to Detroit. You can't send me back there."

"Then why not try to work it out? Let's make a pact right now— you and me against the world. Michael, I saw a marine in Vietnam wearing a flak jacket that said, 'Just you and me, Lord.' You willing to go to war with me? You and me against the world?"

"Yeah, Coach," he said, warming to the idea. "Yeah, I am."

"Here's the deal. You're going to be at *every* workout, *every* class. If you miss a single workout or a single class or any other appointment and I find out about it, it will be you and me against the stadium steps at 5:00 a.m. Loud and clear?"

"Sure, Coach. Loud and clear."

I knew Michael didn't like running stadium steps, but he liked it better than going back to Detroit.

Coach Mac gave us the green light. Two weeks passed, and we stayed connected. Then, in the third week, it happened. He missed a class. I called Michael Westbrook and said, "Tomorrow at the stadium, 5:00 a.m." Just those words and I hung up.

We climbed over the fence to get into the stadium the next morning while it was still dark. We ran them together: twenty-seven flights of stairs, all the way around the stadium. No picnic for him, and it was just about killing me. When we were finished, we climbed into my car and I drove him to his bike. Neither of us spoke a word the entire time.

Two more weeks passed. Michael missed a workout. I made the call. We ran the steps.

Third week, same thing. But now I was getting angry—*I* wasn't the one missing meetings, but I was getting up at four thirty. For the third time, we ran the steps and huffed and puffed over to my car. As I let him out, I spoke for the first time. I said, "Michael, why do you think I'm doing this?"

He looked at the ground and mumbled, "Coach, because you care about me." Then he got on his bike and rode away.

Making the Grade

Michael Westbrook had missed a return to the streets by half an inch—and a few thousand stadium steps. And he had to keep working, nailing down life habits no one had ever taught him.

He was still a sophomore when he approached me one day and said, "Coach, the tutors are making fun of me. They're making me feel stupid. I've got a big exam next week, and I just don't get it."

"What do you think we should do?"

"Could you ask C.J. to help me get ready for the test?"

C.J. was Charles Johnson, a wide receiver who had no problems in the classroom. C.J. was on his way to a graduate degree.

I said, "Sounds like a good idea."

C.J. was happy to help out. So during this time, we took on football and Michael's grades together. For example, there was a big test coming up that would determine his eligibility. Regardless of all our work, if he failed this one, he was out.

By now, in 1992, I was the offensive coordinator. One day at practice I looked toward the gate where the players run onto the field. The academic adviser was heading our way. *Great,* I thought. *They're going to come and yank Michael right off the field in front of his teammates.* I looked over at Michael in the huddle. His eyes were fixed on the counselor.

Michael broke out of the huddle and ran right up to the counselor. He was really worked up. I sent someone in to take his place at wide receiver. When I looked back at the gate, Michael seemed to have lost his mind. He had picked the adviser off the ground and was hugging him for all he was worth, shaking him like a rag doll. It looked as if he were either throttling the counselor or proposing marriage to him. It turned out that he had passed his big test.

After he finished with the adviser, Michael set him down and took off for Coach McCartney and squeezed him with the same energy as he had hugged the academic counselor. Then came me. Then C.J. I was hoping he wasn't going to hug the whole scout team as well.

Actually, I was just as excited; I was finding out that there were experiences in coaching that were even better than winning the games.

During the spring, I was watching ESPN break down the upcoming player draft. The analyst grabbed my attention when he said that the top receiver in the draft would be Michael Westbrook of Colorado—*if* he were eligible to come out, which he wasn't. Michael was only a sophomore! High praise indeed, and I felt as much pride as if they'd said it of me. After all, I had run the stadium steps with him.

The next day, there was Michael at my office door with a huge smile on his face. "Coach, guess what?" He said. "Great news!"

"Come in and sit down," I said, beckoning him to the sofa. "I saw it on television, Michael. Just a sophomore, and already the NFL says you're the man."

Michael looked confused, then disapproving. "What? No, Coach, that's not it! I came to tell you the grades came out. I got all As and Bs! Dean's list! Isn't that great?"

Here was the same young man who had stood in this office with a huge chip on his shoulder and a one-way ticket back to the emptiness of the streets. Now he was a solid student with a much-improved attitude and the National Football League waiting in the wings to make him a millionaire.

Yes, I told myself, *this is what I've been missing all along. It's all about relationships.*

The Last Shall Be First

Our 1992 offense was loaded with talent. We had three future NFL top draft choices in a group that included Kordell Stewart, Michael Westbrook, Christian Fauria, Charles Johnson, and Rae Caruth. Most of them were freshmen or sophomores during my tenure at Colorado.

We had a great group of kids on offense and I worked on building relationships with them all. Christian Fauria, aka Rocky, would go on to win two Super Bowls with the New England Patriots in a long career. Kordell Stewart would play in a Super Bowl his rookie year with the Pittsburgh Steelers, where he would come to be known as "Slash." Michael Westbrook was one of the top five first round picks in 1995 for the Washington Redskins, taken right after Steve McNair from Alcorn State. Charles Johnson, C.J., was also drafted in the first round, also by the Steelers. But Rae Caruth, yet another first round pick, has a sadder story. He was known as "Fever" because of his hot temper. I only wish we could have cured that fever while he was still in Boulder. Rae went on to the Carolina Panthers, had a nice contract and a brilliant career waiting to be fulfilled, and ended up in prison on a murder charge.

This is the other side of the coin when it comes to coaching young men. You do all you can to pour yourself into their lives. There are the feel-good stories of kids such as Michael Westbrook. But there are the others—too many others—who can't handle the power that comes with success, or can't shake free from the bad habits of a past life. They can beat cornerbacks to the end zone, but they can't outrun the invisible enemies that pursue them even after they've seemed to turn the corner in life.

On the playing field itself, things couldn't have gone better. In 1992 we made a radical transition from the wishbone to the kind of wide-open passing attack that was more my specialty. We broke thirty-six school records on our side of the ball. We fell a few yards short of being the second team in NCAA history to have two quarterbacks who both threw for 1,000 yards in a season. In addition to Kordell Stewart, we had a great young freshman named Koy Detmer, who went on to a long NFL career with the Philadelphia Eagles. By now it sounds like football trivia, but we were proud of the goals we reached and exceeded.

We did it all with close-knit guys—an offense young and eager to learn and to lose themselves for the cause of the team. Our team included the walk-ons who showed up for practice without athletic scholarships or much hope for playing time. I hadn't forgotten what that felt like. I made it a special point to treat everyone alike, scholarship and non-scholarship. Everyone who came out and worked up a sweat deserved attention, affirmation, and affection—three needs all young people have.

During spring practice in 1991, one of the other coaches noticed my efforts in that direction. He wanted to know why I was spending extra time at the "jugs" machine that fires balls to the receivers. I was out on the field after most of the kids were in the showers, working with the walk-ons. This coach wanted to know, "What's up with that, Les? Why put in overtime with kids who will never see the field?"

I replied, "They're Colorado Buffaloes, aren't they?"

He shrugged. "Yeah, I guess so."

"Then let's coach 'em."

In the past, it wouldn't have happened. But I was serious about servanthood. I wanted the athletes to see Christ in my life, not in my talk but in my walk. I wanted to be there for them not only on the field but off it, as a friend and counselor.

Years later, in 2004, Chris and I attended the Big XII Championship game between Colorado and Oklahoma in Kansas City. We were walking up the steps when a young man called my name and hurried toward us. It was Jack Keys, one of those dedicated walk-ons at Colorado.

"Hi, Jack," I said. "It's great to see you. It's been a long time."

He gave me a big bear hug and said, "Merry Christmas, Coach Steckel." He asked me what I was doing these days, and I told him I was about to begin a new career as president of Fellowship of Christian Athletes.

Several days later I was back at the FCA office. A staffer looked into my office and said, "We just received a check designated for the support of you and Chris. It's from a guy named Jack Keys. Do you know anything about that?" The amount was a generous one. But what I cared about was the fact that perhaps I had made enough difference in a young man's life that now he wanted to return the favor. Time at the jugs machine was memorable for both of us.

Looking back, I can see the change that had transformed my approach to football. Once these kids had been Xs and Os on the blackboard. Now I saw them as young lives entrusted to me to love and to guide as their coach. Anytime I meet young coaches today, I want them to see what a powerful impact they can have on the young lives before them.

Walking Up the Mountain

When I think back on two happy years in Boulder, it's all about people. Always first were the players. But it was also about the coaches, the high school recruits, the alumni and fans, the trainers and grad assistants. And I can't forget Coach McCartney, whose phone call started it all.

Mac is a man who has walked with God through the high peaks and deep pits of his life. In 1991, of course, I was climbing out of my own darkest and deepest pit just as Mac was entering a time of personal crisis in his career, his family, and his struggle for inner peace.

Coach Mac has already gone on record with the story of his emotional and spiritual journey in the book *From Ashes to Glory* (Thomas Nelson, 1990), and I can't add much to his own moving account. It was a trying time for all of us, but I believe God was working out his own purposes. I know and love Mac, and he will tell you he's a different man today. During my period at Colorado, he was just beginning to work through some of the hurts that permeated his life. He was restless, angry, and very driven. This was a pattern I could recognize from my own life, and we had a number of in-depth, soul-baring conversations. These talks took place during several walks on Fridays, in which we would hike straight up into the mountains and come down again. We had between us a covenant of confidentiality, and each of us identified dark spots within ourselves that we hadn't discovered before. By the time we returned home from those walks, we knew that two driven workaholics had just become a little bit healthier, a little bit closer.

Mac's book details how his inner crisis reached critical mass and how God helped him pick up the pieces. The result was healing in his marriage, his family, and his relationships with people he knew he had hurt. It also came in a decision to walk away from football and devote himself to a new ministry called Promise Keepers. PK has had an extraordinary positive impact on our world, and it rose from the ashes of Coach Mac's terrible pain. All the credit and all the glory go to God. I'm grateful that I could be one very small element in the great mosaic in which God was bringing victory from defeat.

I'm convinced that God's greatest miracles occur in the context of human relationships. I learned that after my time of brokenness. I began to live it out in Colorado, where I learned to be a team player.

The Extra Point

My wife used to tell me this all the time. But as a man, I never listened. The message is that we just can't make it through this life without meaningful relationships. Why is this so difficult for men in particular to understand?

I asked a coach one day, "Who are your closest friends? Do you have two or three?" There was a long pause. He finally looked at me and said, "You know, that's a good question. I'm not sure I have one." How many other men today share that same need for friendship? Far too many.

Life is a full-contact sport. You can't win the game without touching and being touched by others. Today it seems as if most of us have more acquaintances and fewer true friends. Would you mind answering a couple of questions?

- If you were stranded out on a highway somewhere at three o'clock in the morning, how many people do you know who would be willing to come and help you if you called them?
- How many people do you know who can look you in the eye and

tell you the hard truth, particularly when you don't want to hear it?

- How many people can you name who are actively becoming wiser and stronger because of your influence in their lives?

Sure, I know. It takes time to cultivate friendships. Time is gold these days; it's our most precious commodity. And how is it possible for any full-time career person to have twenty or thirty friends?

Forget twenty or thirty. Two or three truly close ones would make a profound difference in your life. Everybody needs one Paul (wise mentor) and one Timothy (young learner) to make them complete. Isn't that what life is all about? Giving and receiving the things that really count.

I travel most of the time these days, and I meet new people every day. Everywhere I go I see men who are tired, angry, and especially lonely. Why is that? Because they are walking down the path alone. There's no reason for anyone to do that. Since we're all heading in the same direction, why not take a few friends along?

8

The Home Team

Up Right Zoom Lee Protection · Cobra

One of the great things about Colorado is skiing, as my wife, Chris, would be sure to tell you. She was coming home from skiing with a friend one day when a little bolt of fear shot through her.

It was about three thirty on a weekday afternoon in early 1993, and my car was at home. This in itself was more unusual than frightening. But the garage door and the car door were both hanging open. Chris figured there must be an emergency with one of the children. She sprinted into the house and up the stairs.

There I was in the bedroom changing clothes. "Honey!" she demanded in panic. "What's wrong?"

"You wouldn't believe it, Prep—Wade Phillips has offered me a job with the Denver Broncos!"

Chris let that sink in, then crashed into me like a free safety on a blitz, knocking me back on the bed. I don't coach defense, but it felt like a pretty sound tackle, fundamentally speaking. Lovingly bone-crushing.

"You told us on Saturday and now it's happening!" she laughed.

She was right—I had called this play in advance. Saturday morning I had risen early, had my devotional time, read my Bible, and prayed. I came away with a very strong impression about the direction of my life. I felt God was telling me that the Broncos were in my future. It was just one of those powerful gut-level convictions we have sometimes. We pray, we reflect upon where we are in life, and some idea suddenly crystallizes.

As I had that feeling of God's leading, of course I was aware that such a feeling is always a subjective thing. It's possible to have the wrong interpretation of such a feeling, though I've had some occasions (such as in the press box at the Music City Miracle) when I was truly certain I had heard God's voice in my life. In this instance, I spent time in prayer and found that I had a clear impression about a future that lay with the Denver Broncos. I believe there are certain times when God pulls the curtain back a few inches and shows us what he has in store; there are other times when we're less sure.

Of course, the thing to do was to follow my prayer-driven hunch and see if the road really led toward Wade Phillips and the Denver Broncos. If Wade had no interest, I would know I'd been mistaken. For the time being, this particular Saturday belonged to my son Christian. We call him C.T. (for Christian Todd). We would watch him play in a junior varsity basketball game, then face off in our annual father-son golf tournament—just the two of us. C.T. would give me thirty strokes (now it's up to forty) and defeat me easily. Golf is his game. I definitely know it's not mine.

After basketball, we were in the parking lot getting ready to move his golf clubs to my car. I stood behind Chris with my hands on her shoulders and said, "Babe, kids, you need to hear this. During my quiet time today, I had a very strong feeling that God was telling me I was heading for a position with the Denver Broncos."

Everyone stood still for a moment. The kids studied me closely, three intense sets of eyes. "Dad, are we going to have to move?"

"I don't think so," I said reassuringly. "Denver is nearby, and it's very possible I could commute, and we could stay right here where we live. Let's just take this one day at a time. I don't have the job yet."

Chris and I had lived in Boulder, San Francisco, Minnesota, Annapolis, New England, and Boulder again. Then there was the constant travel—away games, coaching conventions, and recruiting for the college teams. Chris had always been tremendous about pulling up stakes when it was time to move on. But we were both conscious of the fact that the "home field advantage" was changing with our family.

The kids were beginning to grow up. They were reaching the age where life no longer revolves around Mom and Dad. They were developing their own friends, their own hobbies, and their own roots in the soil of Boulder, Colorado. Their happiness had become an important consideration. It was about all of us now.

But the Lord knows best, and I felt led by him in this instance. Monday morning I had called Wade Phillips at Denver to tell him about my interest. His response: "You're serious?"

"Absolutely."

He said, "I watched your offense at Colorado last season. You're loaded with freshmen and sophomores who are playmakers. Why would you ever want to leave that situation?"

He was right about that. As I've described, we had a roster of future top NFL draft choices at receiver whom we had developed even though they had been recruited for a run-based wishbone offense. It was a nice situation to have, and plenty of coaches would have loved to have had it.

I told Wade, "I just felt led to call you and see if you would have an interest in me."

"Les," he said, "I'd love to hire you. My two openings are with the tight ends and with the running backs. You pick."

I said, "I'll take the tight ends."

"Great," said Wade. "I've got another line ringing. Be here at six tonight and I'll have a contract for you."

The interesting thing was that my old friend John White had played a part in my job change once again—yes, the same John White who had been so persistent in his urging me to talk to Bill McCartney back in 1990. More recently he had called me to say, "Les, I just have a gut feeling you may be headed for the Broncos." He had specified that it wasn't a "spiritual" thing this time, just a good old-fashioned hunch. But now my buddy had a 2–0 record in prophecy!

Sharpening Sharpe

When I think about my time with the Broncos, one player comes particularly to mind. He's an example of why I love coaching and the relationships it makes possible.

Just before I arrived at Denver, I was at a coaching combine in Indianapolis. I ran into Dan Reeves, the former head coach of the Broncos. He had a tip he was eager to pass on to me. "Les, as soon as you get settled in with your new job," he said, "you ought to look out for one particular player. His name is Shannon Sharpe. If you can get him going in the right direction, you'll have something special."

Shannon Sharpe? I hadn't really heard his name. Reeves had drafted him in a late round from Savannah State. He was a tight end who spent time on the developmental squad—an inactive roster player who didn't suit up for games, much like a college walk-on. But I could see the potential. Shannon was sharp mentally with a sense of humor that everybody enjoyed. And when motivated, he had a great work ethic.

The first Wednesday of the regular season, I challenged him. I'd been told he was overdoing the fast food—burgers, fries, shakes. I have always told players that their bodies are the most important asset they have. So I got in Shannon's face and demanded, "How is all that grease and fat going to help you reach your goal to be an All-Pro?" He had no answer.

The greatest thing about Shannon Sharpe was his coachable spirit. From that day on, Shannon became very committed to becoming the best. He worked incessantly in the weight room. He talked to experts on bodybuilding. Before we knew it, his torso was on the cover of fitness magazines. Shannon had become one of the most popular and admired players in the league, with quips and one-liners on every subject. As a player, he was all that Dan Reeves had suggested he could be and more. Shannon would work extra hours on the "jugs" machine until he probably had the best hands in the league. He had an insatiable desire to improve on the finer details of his game. We ran him at tight end, and we spread him out as a wide receiver. While he was on the field, the defense always knew he was a serious threat to account for.

This is what I always loved about coaching—seeing the metamorphosis of a young man from untapped potential to confident achiever, and the friendship that developed through that journey. At the end of the 1993 season, Shannon Sharpe made All-Pro. Heading to the Pro Bowl, he made a typically generous gesture. He gave Chris and me an all-expenses-paid trip to go to the game in Hawaii, as a way of showing his gratitude for my help in reaching his goal. As nice as that was, he kept offering us that same gift for ten years after I left and was no longer coaching. He will never know how much that has meant to my family. As you probably know, Shannon is now a football commentator on television, and he stays busy with a number of other ventures that take advantage of his terrific personality and sense of humor. He's on his way to the NFL Hall of Fame, and no one could deserve it more.

Home and Away

The Broncos position was another one that allowed us to keep the family in place and the kids in their schools. Boulder is a great town, and we all loved it, so I considered it worth a commute to my job in Denver. As it turned out, however, Wade's staff wouldn't be in place for the long term. We made the playoffs in 1993, but in 1994 we got off to a terrible start: four consecutive losses that would ultimately keep us out of postseason play.

At the time, everyone in the organization had their eyes on a hot coaching commodity named Mike Shanahan who had been a popular assistant at Denver. At this point he was coordinating the offense for the San Francisco 49ers. They were loaded with talent on that side of the ball, and he was innovative. The conventional wisdom was that he was waiting in the wings for the Denver head coaching job.

Sure enough, our staff was fired en masse after 1994. But as I was leaving that meeting, an executive came and told me that the owner wanted to see me. It turned out that another assistant and I could keep our jobs. Pat Bowlen, the Bronco owner, told me, "I've been watching you, and I like the way you work with people. Les, there's a job for you here as long as I'm the owner." As you can imagine, hearing those words felt really good. Maybe I had finally succeeded in turning the people skills factor from a deficit to an advantage in my work. I drove home and told my family all about the meeting.

Our kids listened very closely. They had known they might soon be moving to either Jacksonville or Houston, because I had been contacted by the teams there. But now they had fresh hope—Dad could stay with the Broncos and continue to work with one of his favorite players, Shannon Sharpe.

But over the next few days, I began to have nagging doubts about the wisdom of hanging around. When I had become the head coach at Minnesota, I hadn't been allowed to hire all my own assistants. I knew that Mike would feel the same way about that as I had. I said the words one more time: *It's not about me*—not even about Chris or my three kids, really. This was Mike Shanahan's big opportunity. I wanted it to go better for him than it had for me.

So I called Mike and told him it was very important for him to be completely comfortable with his staff. I only wanted to be there if he needed me. Mike really seemed to appreciate my gesture. And after a very positive conversation, we decided the best thing for everyone was for me was to look elsewhere. In the weeks that followed, I had some great conversations with Jeff Fisher, the Oilers' new coach. He made an offer, and I felt that Houston would be the best place for my family. I had only one problem. I still needed a favor from Mike.

"Mike," I asked, "could you leave me a voice mail, explaining the situation so a child could understand it?"

Mike was curious about why I would ask for such a thing.

I said, "I've got a nine-year-old boy at home named Luke, and it's hard for him to see past his friends and his neighborhood and his Little League teams. I would love for him to hear your side of things."

Mike understood, and he left a terrific voice mail on our home phone, carefully explaining his respect for me and how it just wouldn't work out this time. I handed Luke the receiver and said, "Listen to this. See, Coach Shanahan is a nice man. Do you understand?"

Luke said, "Sure, Dad, I understand." And he could see that there were no bad guys in black hats, not even me. We simply had to move on—best for me, best for the Broncos, and we could trust God to make it best for our kids too. But they were at young and tender ages, and we had to help them along gently.

I realized that things had reversed themselves since 1990. The big issue then had been finding a job, and our family was younger and more flexible. Now, at the beginning of 1995, several teams were interested in me, but the home team had become the tricky part. I felt great inner peace and confidence about my career. I had grown to understand that God would always care for our needs. We wanted the kids to understand that he would care for their needs too.

Yet even after Coach Shanahan's gentle call, Luke still had some issues about leaving all his friends in Boulder. As the family packed for Houston, Texas, and our new job with the Oilers, our fourth grader passed a note to his mother announcing that he would proceed with a hunger strike in protest of the move. We kept straight faces the best we could and told him we understood; a kid had to do what a kid had to do.

Luke made a courageous stand for a good hour or two until he saw that the Denver airport had a McDonald's restaurant inside. At that point Luke surrendered to the lure of a Happy Meal. Unfortunately for him, my sister-in-law was present. She ensured that the hunger strike entered the realm of family legend, and Luke is teased about it at every holiday gathering.

Down and Out in Houston

As usual, I didn't wait for the rest of the family. I had moved to Houston in February 1995 and wasted no time getting myself into trouble.

The Oilers' offensive coordinator was Jerry Rhome, and he shared my enthusiasm for basketball. It was only a half-speed pickup game, but we were both competitive. At one point we collided, I slipped, and suddenly I was on the hardwood yelling in pain and pounding the floor. The quadriceps tendon over the top of my kneecap was torn in half. Five days on the job and I was headed for surgery.

The team orthopedic surgeon said it was the second time either he or his dad (also a team doctor) had seen such a tear that extended over the kneecap. Five holes and five high-tech rubber bands later, my leg was back in place. I stayed awake through the whole thing, watching it all. I'm always fascinated with the details by which God has put our bodies together.

Six weeks on crutches followed. There was rehab work with various machines to make sure my knee recovered its flexibility. The staff met every morning at nine, by which time I had been through two and a half hours of personal rehab work.

This is where C.T., our older son, comes into the story. He was a high school junior at the time, and his plans were to come to Texas when the rest of the family made the move. But now things had changed; now his dad needed someone with two good legs and the ability to drive a car.

So C.T. came and helped me for a month. He and I made our temporary home in a hotel room. He would rise early, drop his dad at work, attend his new school, go to golf practice afterward, then pick up his dad and grab some dinner together. Then he would attend an evening class to prepare for the Scholastic Aptitude Test. Finally, he'd hit the sack so he could rise early and take up that whole exhausting regimen all over again.

It was quite a life and quite a sacrifice for a seventeen-year-old guy. Did C.T. complain? No, because he was happily focused on golf. In Colorado, it was an autumn game like football. In Texas, they played it in the spring. Coming to the Lone Star state meant that C.T. could be on the green several months early, which was fully okay with him. Not only that, now his dad could see him play because I was much more available during the spring—our off-season.

This was a great time of bonding with my teenage chauffeur and dinner companion. And it wasn't long before his high school golf team went to the state championship tournament in Austin. I was absolutely thrilled to see my son play golf for the first time, with our seasons not conflicting.

As I walked the course with all the other proud parents, I began to think about my three very special kids and the little things that make each one unique.

49ers Baby

C.T. is our oldest, a "49ers baby" born during our first days in NFL coaching. There has always been an intensity about his presence that comes through his blue eyes. When he was just a little boy, he played "Coach" by dressing up in a team sweater and stereo headphones with a toothbrush taped to the headset. In his imaginary world, he was calling plays from the sideline. But that pretend microphone now seems more than a bit prophetic. As he grew older, he would provide tongue-in-cheek play-by-play coverage of family events in the style of TV sportscasters. He has been smart, articulate, and quick with words from the beginning. It's no surprise that he has chosen television sports journalism as a career. At this writing, he covers UCLA and Southern Cal for Fox Sports Net in Los Angeles. A real mike has replaced the toothbrush.

Growing up, C.T. found that being a coach's son had its perks. When we would move to a new city and a new neighborhood, word would get around that a "football guy" had bought that house down the block. Boys thought that was cool, so C.T. had no problems making friends. On the other hand, he knew he could be forced to move away from them at any time, so to a certain extent he was careful about getting too close. He focused on athletics and academics and always did well. But as a newcomer, he was always finding that he had to work harder to earn his place.

C.T. started with tennis and baseball, moved to basketball on the strength of a killer jump shot, and then, at twelve, found his great sporting passion: golf. It was love at first putt. Chris's parents gave him his first clubs, and our son quickly became a student of the game. His focus and passion for this newfound sport helped him improve dramatically over a relatively short time. What counted was that he was blazing a new trail, because golf was a game I'd never made time to master. C.T. had found a niche where he could make his own name. Before we knew it, he was involved in national junior tournaments and ultimately earned a golf scholarship to Vanderbilt University in Nashville, Tennessee.

Not that he was trying to distance himself in any way. C.T. was proud and protective of everyone in our family, and it was he who was perhaps the most sensitive to media criticism of his dad's job performance. He had my back all the time, even (without my permission!) on talk radio. C.T. would listen to the local sports stations doing their standard, critical armchair quarterbacking. He would create various identities and call the show to defend my offensive philosophy, picking apart their comments using the X-and-O details he had learned in a coaching family. The radio personalities would be shocked. Who *was* this caller? I was less than pleased, of course. What if the station traced the call? Secretly I felt the pride any dad feels when his children love and support him.

C.T. took his golfing to the next level. He transferred from Vanderbilt to Baylor University in Waco, Texas. After finishing there, he headed to California to try to earn his tour card. I was encouraging him to pursue his dreams while he was young—to live his life with no regrets. But after a year, he decided that the sacrifices and the lifestyle weren't for him. It was even more traveling than he had grown up with. So he moved into sports journalism. C.T. makes wise decisions and knows where he's going, every inch his own man. Our oldest son has a bright future ahead. I've given up any hope of ever beating him at golf, but that's fine as long as he stays off those talk radio stations!

Viking Baby

When C.T. was three and I was an assistant in Minnesota, we added a daughter to our little family—the other "Les" in the family. It's always amazing how different two kids can be. Where C.T. is intense, certain, generally black-and-white in his perceptions, Lesley is softer, a bit more social, and tuned into the gray areas of life; fair-haired and fair-minded.

An amazing people person, Lesley was quick to find a "new best friend" at the hotel pool as we traveled to away games. When our team struggled or I lost a position, Lesley was optimistic and resilient, always seeing the bright side, always assured that good times were just around the corner. I realized early on that it could be a challenge for a daughter in a football family. C.T. and Luke could come into the locker room after a game and get into the middle of the action. Chris and Lesley had to wait patiently outside.

Yet Lesley loved being a coach's daughter, identifying with the team, wearing the team colors, doing the road trips, cheering us on. That show-and-tell session in fifth grade didn't hurt either. For her segment, she brought a group of Colorado Buffaloes into the classroom: Kordell Stewart, Koy Detmer, Christian Fauria, Michael Westbrook, and others. It was a fifth grade smash. "*That* was the greatest show-and-tell in the history of school," she said with satisfaction afterward.

I took her on "dinner dates" without the two boys. We let her be a girl. In high school, she was voted "most school-spirited" and had the honor of singing in Carnegie Hall in New York with the school chorus. Her mother traveled with the group, I flew in for the performance, and for once there was Lesley in the spotlight and her parents in the crowd. She said, "This was my Super Bowl."

Lesley did find moving to be a challenge, as all my kids did. Especially at younger ages, some girls can be cliquish. Lesley's new classmates weren't so likely to be impressed with football credentials in the way C.T's and Luke's friends were. Some of them weren't interested in inviting a new friend into their groups. Lesley, being as social as she was, struggled at times with the feeling of exclusion. There was pressure in high school to make poor choices in order to earn peer acceptance. But inner strength always guided her way.

We often recall one event that helps us remember how hard this life can be for children. When we moved from New England to Colorado in 1991, it was spring break. That's the usual timing for a move in an NFL family. A few weeks after we arrived, there was a springtime field day in Lesley's class, with all kinds of games and relays. Chris was watching from the side with all the other parents when she noticed that Lesley could not find a partner for the three-legged race. One girl would tell her, "I already have a partner." Another would simply say, "I don't want to be your partner." A third would quickly get someone else rather than pair up with this new girl.

Chris was horrified. The tears swelled behind her sunglasses as she watched her daughter face rejection over and over again. She thought, *Is this what we put our children through with each new job?* The teacher wasn't particularly interested in helping until Chris insisted that Lesley needed to have a partner—*and fast.* All the same, Chris couldn't help but notice how resilient her daughter was. Lesley never drew back and felt sorry for herself. She just kept approaching different girls and asking politely if each one would be her partner.

That's Lesley—mentally tough yet hanging on to a tremendous heart for the underdog, the kid who is left out. To this day she loves working with kids and is preparing to teach school. She'll be that outstanding teacher, a coach in her own right, who sees that no child is left behind.

But I have to tell one more Lesley story. We were riding home in the car after a tough loss in an NFL game. It was a critical situation in the game, and our team came up short. The whole family was in the car, nursing our disappointment, when Lesley broke the silence: "Dad, can I ask you a question?"

"Sure."

"You know that third down call you made—the draw play?"

"Yes," I said.

"What were you thinking?"

That's coaching; everyone's a critic. Later a brother whispered to her with an elbow in her ribs, "I can't *believe* you questioned Dad's play-calling!"

But it's okay, because the way I see it, Lesley has earned that right by surviving and thriving as a coach's daughter. She's an absolute delight.

Patriot Baby

Finally, meet Luke, our youngest, who came into the world during our first Super Bowl year in New England. An easygoing and quick-witted little brother, Luke always kept his older siblings guessing—and entertained. His unique distinction is that he has managed to break more bones (of his own, that is) than any member of the family.

Yet when it comes time to be serious, Luke has always been able to focus on a goal. Once he decides his destination, no one will outwork him on his way there. His unique combination of giftedness and determination means that he'll be a high achiever in whatever direction he chooses. Today he's a student–athlete at Princeton University and a linebacker on its football team. As we were working on these paragraphs,

Luke called to talk about his team's thrilling win over Ivy League power Penn that weekend. He had his big moment when a teammate blocked a Penn extra-point kick that would have cut Princeton's lead in half. Luke scooped up the ball and set out for the far end zone, looking over his shoulder for a faster teammate more capable of outrunning the pursuers. When that teammate ran up, Luke flipped him the ball. But he did so in the stylish manner of a quarterback option pitch—a fact not lost on his teammates, who kidded him afterward. That's Luke: alert, hard-charging, getting it done with a flourish. As he enters his senior year, his teammates have elected him defensive captain.

Luke definitely has his own approach to everything, including the challenges of a coach's family. C.T. focused on golf and avoided the deeper friendships that might have been harder to give up during the next move. Lesley plunged right in and cultivated all the friendships she could. As for Luke, it was his way to spend plenty of time studying the lay of the land, socially speaking. He never opened himself until he was sure who the "real" friends were—the ones worth taking the time to get to know. Once he made a friend, he was a friend for life, establishing a friendship more durable than the moving van.

But that didn't make the moves any easier for Luke. I've shared how I asked Mike Shanahan to leave a voice mail for him, helping him understand why a move was the right solution. We didn't know at the time that our son's anguish would be deeper and more poignant with a future move. Nor could we guess that God would use Luke's grief to teach our family a lesson we'll never forget.

There's absolutely nothing in life like the togetherness of a family. You feel it at Thanksgiving or Christmas, or when casually looking at pictures of old family vacations: so much accumulated history together, so much growth, so much learning. These are the people who matter most in the whole world. You'd give your life for them without even stopping to think.

A family has that fit that's just right. A running joke of ours was imagining the five of us as a basketball team. Everyone agreed that Chris was the center, the MVP, the "playmaker" around whom all the action revolved. C.T. had to be the shooting guard; after all, in real life he had a terrific jump shot. I was the point guard, bringing the ball up court and calling the plays. Lesley was the power forward because she was always assertive, in the lanes of life, mixing it up with everybody. Luke was "the other forward," the youngest, the last to join the team and therefore getting last choice of bedrooms in each new house.

But I think we were onto something. A good basketball team has amazing chemistry. A guard can make a no-look pass because he knows the movements of his teammates almost instinctively. Everyone is in sync, working together, using his or her different skills, making sacrifices, doing what it takes to win. A family is at least intended to function in the same way: through how we support one another, the whole becomes greater than the sum of its parts. And if we go about it selfishly, the whole team fails to function.

I couldn't be more pleased by the versatile team of five we have become. As I grow older, I think more and more about my legacy— about the influence I leave behind. I once thought it might have something to do with wins on a football field or a head coaching résumé. Now I realize that it has do with what I accomplish for the kingdom of God. I also understand that a great part of my legacy is what my children accomplish in this world, far into the future. I believe that God has a plan and a purpose for each of our children. If they continue to follow him, the impossible could become possible in their lives.

The Extra Point

Psalm 127:3–5 says, "Children are a gift from the LORD; they are a reward from him. Children born to a young man are like sharp arrows in a warrior's hands. How happy is the man whose quiver is full of them!" I love that picture of the warrior-dad, firing those arrows far into tomorrow, beyond even our own field of vision. Your children extend the range of your impact on this world and its future. Have you ever thought about that?

Men often tell me they dream of coaching—but how many get the chance? I tell them that there is no man anywhere who doesn't have a golden opportunity to coach, if he is a husband or a father. You can win something more than an athletic contest. You can win the hearts and minds of the children who count on you for guidance and love. God has gently placed them in your keeping, and there is no nobler task in all this world than that of being a wise and loving parent.

Are you pouring attention, affirmation, and affection into your family? Are you helping your children to be the very best they can be; to set worthy goals within their sights; to have a firm awareness that they are loved, so that one day they will be able to begin loving families of their own? Coaching a football team is a nice career for some. Coaching our children is a calling for all of us.

If you're a parent, consider your relationship with the children God has given you. Know that each one of them is a first-round pick, uniquely selected by the Creator for your home team. Every one of them has the potential to grow, develop, and shine, just as Shannon Sharpe did. What can you do to encourage them today?

Coach 'em up, Coach!

9

You Make the Call

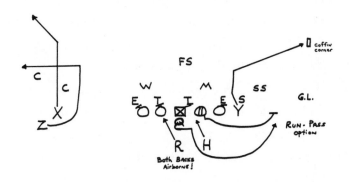

The idea of working with Tony Dungy had always appealed to me. It seemed like a perfect fit.

For one thing, Tony was a winner. He had quickly become the most successful Tampa Bay head coach ever, an NFL Coach of the Year. His Buccaneer teams, known for their intimidating defenses, played sound, fundamental football. There were two factors in particular that attracted me to working for Tony: one, he was a devout Christian; two, he was in need of an offense as dynamic as his defense.

Like me, he had learned the ropes of NFL football in Minnesota. His success running their defense earned him a chance as head coach in Tampa Bay. When word came that Tony would be looking for an offensive coordinator, I knew it would be wise to explore the possibility. It was early in the year of 2000, a new decade, a new millennium. And our Titans team had just been to the Super Bowl.

We were at the Phoenician, a resort in Scottsdale, Arizona, when the possibility suddenly entered our lives. After the city of Nashville honored the Titans with a parade and stadium celebration, Chris and I were standing in the stadium tunnel waiting to be introduced to the fans when quarterback Neil O'Donnell and his wife, Leslie, began kidding me. Neil was saying, "Hey, Cheapskate, why not take your wife somewhere nice for a change? Why not spend some of that bonus money and have some fun?"

The O'Donnells recommended the Phoenician Resort, so that's where we went. The only problem was that I couldn't get Chris to go out to dinner. She was glued to ESPN and its coverage of the Pro Bowl, the NFL postseason all-star game in Hawaii. "They're going to interview Eddie George," she would say. Or it was Bruce Matthews. Or Frank Wycheck. Prep can't stand to miss a single thing when it comes to her sports viewing, not even the interviews.

I was in a hurry to meet Ed Rush and his wife, Trudy, for dinner. Ed is a close friend who was the director of officiating for the National Basketball Association. I looked at my watch and told Chris we could wait another minute or two.

But this happened for four nights. "Babe," I said, "they've interviewed everyone but the trainers. Come on, let's get some dinner."

"Just another minute."

That's when the announcement was made that Dungy had fired his offensive coordinator.

Chris said, "Honey, you've always said you'd like to work with Tony Dungy."

I just looked at her and shrugged. She was right, but I had a job. Of course I would be rehired in Nashville, but the fact was that my contract was expiring on February 15, and the re-signing process was typically slow.

I did something I'd never done before. I hired an agent, Larry Thrailkill, a terrific attorney who happened to be my Sunday school teacher at Brentwood Baptist Church outside Nashville. As a matter of fact, I refused to miss his class even on game days when we were playing in Nashville. That's not a typical thing in NFL life. I would hurry from church to the stadium, and the players would give me a hard time: "Well, it must be time to tee it up. Les is here."

Larry knew his way around the league. He had actually been the general manager of the San Francisco 49ers for a few months. So for legal, spiritual, and football reasons, he was the perfect choice.

I felt it wise to hire an agent because I was seeing a lot of coaches handled unfairly by management in the league. Some teams would extend the process of contract negotiation right up to the season, but the coach had no safety net. I didn't look forward to all that uncertainty, so I had mentioned to Larry that if we didn't have a contract in hand by mid-February, we would have to consider other opportunities.

Of course, I was at a career high point, having just coached in the Super Bowl. I knew I could get a job somewhere else if for some reason I wasn't valued in Nashville. We loved it there, loved the team, and enjoyed working for Jeff Fisher. We hoped to stay. We simply wanted some security and a fair salary based on league standards.

Contract Confusion

I was driving home from the office one night in mid-February when I felt a spiritual impulse to call Tony Dungy. I was stunned by the sudden thought and wondered, *Where did this come from?* I called Larry, shared the thought with him, and asked for an update on our contract negotiations. He said, "We're at a standstill," he said. "No activity at all with your contract."

Within a few days my contract expired and the Titans had made no move. I wanted to go through the proper channels, so I had Larry call the league office in New York City to clear me to talk to other teams. On February 16, I called Tampa and left a message for Tony.

He soon called back and said, "Hi, Les, what can I do for you?"

"Tony, I felt led to give you a call," I said. "I'd like to know if you're interested in exploring the possibility of hiring me as your offensive coordinator."

Silence met my ears.

"Tony? You still there?"

"I'm sorry, Les."

"Is this a bad time?"

"No, I'm just in shock. Les—you're not under contract with the Titans?" He couldn't understand how that could be true after such a strong season in Nashville.

"No, I'm not. It's okay for us to talk. I have an agent, and he's cleared it with New York."

Silence again, then, "Les, I was just thinking about what happened to me yesterday."

"What was that?"

"I had interviewed three people in the last few weeks and narrowed it down to two. Just the other day I gave them both my word that I would call them at noon today with my decision."

"And?"

"Les. Look at your watch."

I looked. "Ten fifty-five."

"Central time, yeah. But it's an hour later where I am," he said. He had come to within five minutes of hiring someone else.

Tony made a couple of calls, then we talked again. He wanted me to fly down to see him. Larry told me to do it quietly. He advised me to call once I was in Florida. "If you call them now, they'll block your driveway," he said. "You'll never get to Tampa."

I wanted to do the right thing. I really like Jeff Fisher, as well as the coaches, players, and fans in Tennessee. Everyone had been good to me. I called Jeff from the airport in Miami, where we were changing planes. The whole thing took him by surprise; management handled contracts, so he had no idea there was a possibility I could leave. "I've always been able to trust you, Les," he said. "Would you promise me you won't sign anything?"

"You have my word," I said.

I know Jeff talked to some of the coaches after our conversation. He visited with Sherman Smith, our running backs coach and one of my best friends, to get his thoughts. "Tony Dungy and Les Steckel— that's a match made in heaven," Sherm said. He knew that faith was important to both of us.

I met with Tony and interviewed, but there was no offer at that point. I flew home exhausted after weather delays at the Atlanta airport.

Early the next morning I heard the front door slam as Luke ran outside to catch his ride for school. I went to the kitchen to find Chris visibly upset. "What is it, Prep?" I asked. "What's wrong?"

Chris said, "Look at the paper."

The newspaper was folded to the headline, "Steckel Talks to Tampa Bay; Offensive Coordinator Probably Won't Be Back."

I was surprised that the word had leaked out, and I went to the office to visit with Jeff. We shared what had transpired over the last twenty-four hours. Jeff had been taken off guard by the statement that I was leaving, and he was also under the impression that I'd already signed an agreement in Florida. I quickly corrected him.

"What?" he asked. "They didn't give you a contract?"

"Remember, Jeff? I gave you my word I wouldn't sign anything."

"Did they offer you a job?"

"Not yet. Tony wanted to pray about it."

We continued to talk for a while, and we agreed to wait and see how events played out. As the day moved on, I was even contacted by a third NFL team. I was a little embarrassed by all the media attention. I knew that I had to walk through this confusing situation to see what God had in store for us.

It wasn't long before Tony called and made us an offer. Chris and I both felt God's leading to accept it. That afternoon we broke the news to Luke when he came home after school that we were, in fact, making another move. Our son was fourteen by this time, and he'd really settled into Nashville life. His middle school football team had gone undefeated. He had a great group of friends, all of them excited about moving on to Brentwood High together. Luke had really come into his own at this stop along our family's journey.

Therefore, after the "playoffs or pink slips" publicity, Luke had prayed hard for the Titans to win enough games that his family would not have to move. And with a Super Bowl appearance, it seemed to him that God had come through in a big way. Everyone in the city was buzzing about the Titans, and his dad was one of the coaches. He had felt secure; now he was devastated.

Chris and I tried to explain all the complicated developments. I told Luke that Mom and I had prayed about it and felt that it was God's will that we take the job with the Bucs.

Luke listened incredulously as we talked about being obedient to God. He shouted, "What kind of God do you serve?"

What could we say? Luke had prayed, and it almost seemed to him as if God had given him what he asked, then taken it back.

Luke said, "We made the Super Bowl, Dad, and you're making me move again? I don't know what God you're praying to, but my God isn't listening." He bolted up the stairs and slammed his bedroom door. Luke was far more than disappointed; he was deeply angry—at me, at football, and at God. This was his time to celebrate. He had made all the moves with his family. He had taken the hits. His team had finally gone to the Big One, and he didn't even have time to enjoy the aftermath of a Super Bowl season—walking down the hall in school wearing his new Super Bowl gear and all those other shining moments a teenager would savor.

Chris and I understood what Luke was feeling. We had our own fears for him—what kind of school could we find? Who would be his new friends? How could we replace that ideal situation in which he had thrived in Brentwood?

We made the decision to let him finish out the school year, to give him time to say his good-byes and acclimate himself to the reality of leaving. It looked like a miserable summer for him in Tampa when his heart was somewhere else. That's why it was touching to see his big sister change her own summer plans. Lesley was at Baylor University, and she had looked forward to spending her summer as a counselor at Kamp Kanakuk in Branson, Missouri. But she cut her time short to come stay in Tampa so Luke would have "someone to hang out with."

Leaving Tennessee was tough on all of us, but I had to make the call. If God was leading us to a new situation, as Chris and I believed, then he would care for our family. We've all felt the way Luke did, as though "my God isn't listening." We have to push forward and trust that in the long run, we'll understand.

In this case, we ultimately found out just how true that principle could be.

High Hopes

Here were the Tampa Bay Buccaneers, a team eager for greatness. In 1999 they had come tantalizingly close to going the distance. They'd lost to the St. Louis Rams 11–6 in the NFC Championship, then stayed home to watch us play one of the greatest Super Bowls ever. When you give up only eleven points and lose in a championship game, it's natural to say, "What can we do to make the offense more prolific?"

The x-factor to the upcoming season was that Super Bowl XXXV would be played at Raymond James Stadium in Tampa. The fans were caught up in a vision of what it would be like to play in a Super Bowl with a home field advantage.

Therefore, there was a powerful mandate in Central Florida. It was time to go all the way. Simply add a high octane offense to the present intimidating defense, and a championship had to follow, right?

On March 1, 2000, I moved to an Embassy Suites hotel in the Tampa Bay area. I made my headquarters there until Chris and Luke could follow me. I can remember piles of papers all over the bed and the floor as I tried to put in a totally new offense. I often fell asleep right where I lay, on the floor among all those scattered pages. I needed to fine-tune an offense I knew well but one I could teach quickly to the assistants currently on Tony's staff. When practice began, the offensive staff and the players got a cram course that required everyone to hit the ground running. But camp went well, preparation went well, and the season could not have possibly gotten off to a more powerful start.

Maybe it was too good to be true. The home-field Super Bowl theme became bigger than ever. The fans could practically taste it. I was the guy coming in from a team that had been there, so our offense was a popular media topic. I received constant requests for television interviews and radio appearances.

I was very uncomfortable about the extra attention. I knew it wasn't about me. I went to the defensive coach and let him know that all the publicity was definitely not my idea. He was doing a great job with the defense. I even went to Tony Dungy at one point and asked him not to give me a game ball again, as he had done after a big offensive explosion. This was about a *team,* and we didn't need to create any resentment. But all the hoopla continued as we won our first three games. We beat Chicago 41–0 and Detroit 31–10. C.T. flew in for the Chicago game and told me at dinner, "Dad, win this one and it's your two hundredth victory." It was news to me—I never kept track. He was counting college games, pro games, the whole thing.

Winning makes people happy. I even received a phone call from the wife of one of the defensive assistants, just telling me how thrilled she was to have Chris and me on the team. It seemed to me that everything was right on track for a huge season.

Then, right out of the blue, the bottom fell out.

Our Bucs lost four straight games in the middle of the season, including a loss by fourteen to the same Detroit team we had beaten by twenty-one. Somehow we lost to Chicago on the road after beating them by forty-one points at home. What was going on? The city experienced a tremendous emotional mood swing from delight to devastation. Some grumbling and finger-pointing began to break out on the team.

One quiet Saturday morning I was busily at work in my tiny office, just off the locker room, when I kept hearing a strange noise at the door. I finally got up and opened the door, and there stood a little boy of about six. I smiled because I recognized him as the son of our video director—the man who films our practices and games.

He looked up at me and said, "Coach Steckel, did you see the paper this morning?"

"No, I didn't."

He said, "Oh, okay," and just like that, he was gone.

His visit seemed very strange, almost as if the little boy had a message to deliver. I called home to check in with Chris and asked her if she'd read the morning paper.

"I'm afraid I did," she replied.

I said, "So what's up?"

One of our biggest stars from the defensive side had ripped me in the paper. And practice was just about to start. When I got out to the field, you might have thought I had leprosy. No one wanted to look me in the eye. No one even wanted to be within five yards of me. Apparently everyone on the team was a newspaper reader.

Sudden Death

Still, we won seven of the last ten games, and in the process we set a number of team offensive records. Those who have played for me know that I place a tremendous emphasis on avoiding turnovers, scoring in the red zone, and eliminating penalties. If ever there was anything I programmed into my players, it was to lock away the ball so it wouldn't be fumbled. Some players today love to carry it in one hand for the showmanship value. Not while I'm coaching. We had the fewest fumbles and tied for the fewest interceptions in franchise history. We set franchise records that still stand for touchdowns, for most points scored in a season, and for most yards rushed in a game. In the end the team had won ten of sixteen in the regular season. It was that one slump that really hurt us, particularly in terms of team chemistry.

By any normal standards, it was a successful season in the NFL, with a big upgrade in the team's offense. Yet there was one standard for measurement that year among Tampa Bay fans. When the Super Bowl kicked off in Raymond James Stadium, the Buccaneers were supposed to be on the field. But we lost in the wild card round on New Year's Day 2001 against the Eagles in Philadelphia. Our offense was dismal, we didn't play well, and I felt totally responsible. The season was over, and the Super Bowl dream was extinguished.

It was a frustrating time to be a coach. I remember driving home each day, trying to keep my spirits up by listening to tapes of Charles Stanley preaching about "advancing through adversity." Who would have thought I'd be back in such a situation a year after the Super Bowl?

After our final loss to Philadelphia, one week passed. On a Monday afternoon, I was in my office when Tony Dungy stopped by. He came into my office and sat down. He said, "Les, we're going to have to let you go."

I said, "You're kidding."

He said, "No."

I was trying to take it in. This was like a thunderbolt on a clear day—totally unexpected.

I said, "Did you pray about this?"

"Yes."

I said, "Tony, did you pray long and hard about this?"

He said, "Yes."

"Okay, then, I accept it. I just know God has a plan."

Tony is a great guy and a strong Christian. He's still a close friend. I know he didn't want to fire me, but he faced a no-win situation in which he had to make a move. He took a hard look at his options, prayed about them, and made his decision. I'm sure he felt that, with my experience in the league, I could land another job—in other words, that God would have better things in store for us. He was more right about that than he could have known.

Making Our Move

As we continued to talk about my leaving, I shared with Tony some of my worries about our house. It's amazing how your mind can move from the emotional to the practical in a moment. The reality of the challenges of this business was all too familiar. In accepting this job, I'd rushed down to Tampa from Nashville to get an early start. We'd bought a house that happened to have plenty of cracked tiles leading from the entryway through the kitchen. It seemed like a small thing, but we had no time to fix it. We were told there were replacement tiles in the attic, but they didn't match and the pattern was obsolete.

We simply covered the tiles with rugs, but now they would be a tremendous obstacle to selling the house. I asked myself, "Who is going to buy a house with broken tiles?"

Another move was hard to even think about; a real estate obstacle was the last thing we needed.

When I got home, I saw Luke, who had suffered so much over this move. He had made the adjustment, but he'd kept up with his Nashville friends through instant messaging. He told us that he had actually grown closer than ever to the guys back in Brentwood. I waited until he left the room, then told Chris, "Honey, they just fired me."

Chris was even more shocked than I'd been: "You're kidding!"

I told her I was very serious.

She said again, "You're kidding." I'd been fired before, but this time it made no sense at all. The newspaper had just run a story about our having "the most prolific offense in franchise history." Chris was totally blindsided by the news. Luke later told us that it was the most pain he had ever seen in his mother's face.

The three of us drove over to the team headquarters and worked until two in the morning to clear out my office. Luke still talks about how surreal it seemed, the dark rooms that were usually so loud and so lively. He was used to hanging out in the locker room, my tiny office, and all the places associated with the adrenaline rush of pro football. Now the lights were off and no one but us was there. We didn't break the silence at all but went about packing and organizing without speaking a word.

We were working through our shock and processing our emotions about the crisis. We pointed to boxes, handed each other packing tape, helped carry things, and uttered not a word.

Raymond's Wisdom

Two weeks later, my old friend and mentor Raymond Berry called to find out how I was doing.

"Well," I said, "I guess we're still in shock."

He said, "Listen, Les. I've been coaching and playing football all my life. My dad was a coach. I know how things work, and I understand that this is about personalities. The secular world is confused because of the success you had down there. The Christian community is confused because of the friendship you have with Tony. That's how I know God is involved in this thing. And I want you to tell me what's going on."

I didn't respond, not really knowing what to say.

"Les," he said firmly, "I want names."

I tried to explain the situation in more general terms, but he insisted. "I want every name," he said.

I held the phone away from my face and said to my wife, "I'm not sure this is Raymond!" I said to the phone, "Raymond, this is you, right?"

"It's me."

"Then why would you want names?"

"Because I'm going to pray for every single one of those people. And I expect you to pray for them too. Furthermore, I want you to read the Psalms every day for at least this next year. They'll help to heal your spirit."

I agreed to his strict orders and began to share with him the little I knew. Then he said good-bye and hung up.

I understood Raymond's wisdom. He knew that there was no damage others could do to me that would be worse than the damage I would inflict on myself through bitterness. I took his advice. I prayed regularly for these men and trusted God to have a plan for my future. God had already begun to answer our prayers.

The day after the firing, we were watching ESPN when the update ticker of crawling news and scores read "Tampa Bay Fires Offensive Coordinator Les Steckel." It's never too enjoyable to have your life's lowlights headlined for the world to read. But that afternoon the phone rang. Our realtor wanted to express her regrets about the news and tell us that the folks who sold us the house wanted to buy it back, if it was for sale.

We were astounded. There was our answer. Who would buy a house with broken tiles but the people who sold it to you? The real lesson, of course, was bigger than that. The bottom line on ESPN may deliver bad news, but the bottom line of trusting God is that he will always care for you. Once again we could see his fingerprints—this time on a series of cracked tiles in a home we needed to leave behind.

Don't Blow the Call!

Within two weeks of the firing, I had an offensive coordinator job offer from another team. That was gratifying. In such a hurtful situation, we have a natural eagerness to rebound quickly. We want to seize the reins of another job and show the world that we're still on top, that we're bigger than our latest misfortune. That's how I had felt after the Vikings fiasco in 1984. Just give me a shot, and I'll show 'em!

That was then; this is now. In my heart I wanted to get right back to coaching in the NFL. But in a deeper place in that same heart, I wanted to do what was right for others—particularly my family.

I had once made a promise to my children that they would go to no more than two high schools in four years. Any more transition than that was simply too much to ask of a young person. And here we were with our first true test of my rule: Luke was a high school freshman in Brentwood, Tennessee; he was a sophomore at Berkeley Prep in Tampa; and now he would be a junior in a third city, if I accepted that job—Luke, of all people, who had been so reluctant to leave his Brentwood friends behind. He had given all that up for this one year in Florida, and were we now going to drag him to yet another city?

I had made the rule limiting the moves, and by that rule, a move was out.

Chris and the kids were supportive. They knew I needed to coach. They said, "He who makes the rules can break the rules." But I knew it was time to step up to the plate and do the right thing instead of the easy thing. I had always said my priorities were faith, family, and football—in that order. I wasn't about to switch the positions of the last two. Yes, the more I thought about it, the more clearly I understood what was right.

I decided not to coach for a year and furthermore to move back to Brentwood where Luke could rejoin his old school and his old friends. I had been away from my family for three months when I came to Tampa Bay early and stayed in a hotel. Then, during the season, I had worked so hard that we'd hardly seen each other. I felt that God was saying, "Les, this is your family's time. Give yourself to them now."

As an offensive coach and game planner, my career has always been about making the right call. Pass or run? Sideline or over the middle? Strong side or weak side? I've spent countless hours creating a game plan, only to have the game come down to one play call, as it did in Super Bowl XXXIV. As a coach, you make the call and you live with the results.

I look back now on the Tampa Bay episode of my life and I see that it was all about making tough calls. First there was the decision to leave a good situation in Nashville and follow God's direction to Tampa. Then there was the decision about whether to be bitter when I faced adversity. If I'd given in and been sidetracked by anger, I surely would have blown the third big call. That was the one about whether to honor my commitment to my family.

I can't say I have a flawless record as a play-caller, either on the football field or on the field of life. I've made some poor calls, to be sure. But I hope that as the years have gone by, they've brought a bit of wisdom. I called these "plays" during this crucial period of my life:

- to follow God rather than stay inside my comfort zone,
- to forgive those who fired me rather than hang on to bitterness, and
- to father first and coach second.

Thinking back, I realize how easy it is for one bad call to roll into another. If I had done the wrong thing on that second one, and clung to bitterness, I surely would have blown the next one as well, because I would have rushed into another job and risked doing the wrong thing as a father.

Our year with the Bucs could be summarized this way:

On March 1, 2000, I moved to Tampa alone.

On March 1, 2001, we moved back to Tennessee—together.

We simply wanted to be a family and to be faithful. But the best was yet to come.

The Extra Point

All this talk about "making the right call" is just another way of talking about priorities, isn't it? When I speak about faith, family, and football, it's the same thing.

Priorities. It's a great buzzword, the kind of thing we throw around without thinking too much about it. Every one of us, for example, would say that we would put people before career. But let me ask you something: Would your last five decisions, large or small, confirm that statement of priorities? When you have a choice to make in terms of how to spend your time, do your loved ones consistently come before your work?

Every decision you make is a play call—a mini mission statement about what is important to you in life. What makes you the happiest in life?

If you had to give up people, places, and things one by one until you got down to the bare essentials, what would go first? What would go last?

It comes down to the issue of what you consider to be your treasure. Jesus said, "Wherever your treasure is, there your heart and thoughts will also be" (Matt. 6:21).

I challenge you today to go on a treasure hunt. Find out what treasures lay in your heart, and determine which are the most precious of all. Then align your life accordingly. No, it's not as simple as it sounds. It can be very difficult at times, as it was for me when I decided not to coach for a period of time. But in the end, it's the greatest way to build integrity into your life.

Stop and ask yourself these questions:

- When God speaks, do you listen?
- When God commands, do you obey?
- When God leads, do you follow?

You make the call.

10

This Is Your Life

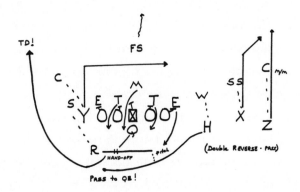

POWER LEFT "FRIDAY NIGHT SPECIAL"

Life was wide open during the spring of 2001. I had turned down an offensive coordinator position just two weeks after my dismissal so that Luke could finish high school with his friends in Brentwood, just south of Nashville. He was thrilled to be going back. So were we.

Prior to closing on our Tampa house and finding a home in our old neighborhood in Brentwood (another of God's major provisions), I had to figure out what to do with all the empty time.

One day while we were still in Tampa, the phone rang. I heard a thick-as-molasses Southern drawl on the other end of the line.

The voice said, "Howdy, Les. It's Jack Daniels from Tennessee." What a classic name: Jack Daniels, and he lives in Tennessee.

"Les," he continued, "I'm still the football coach at Brentwood High School. I hear you're headin' back this way."

"That's right," I said. Jack had heard the news from some of our Tennessee friends.

"Well, how'd you like to be a volunteer coach for our Bruins?"

"Well, Jack, I don't know about that," I replied.

"You'd qualify," he said. We laughed, and I told him his offer would have to be a matter for prayer.

Meanwhile, we made our move to Brentwood. I walked the dog four times a day. I had two-hour daily workouts instead of my usual one-hour workouts. A few buddies at the gym began calling me "Mayor of the Brentwood YMCA." At night we'd catch a movie, usually recommended by Luke, our family's movie buff. But as a man accustomed to sixteen- to eighteen-hour workdays, I knew that the life of leisure might just drive me crazy.

Chris and I continued to pray about Jack Daniels' offer, and I even did my homework. Our friend Thom Park from Pensacola had done this very thing, volunteer-coaching his son's team. We asked him to talk to us about the pros and cons of such an opportunity. Our hesitation involved the fact that this was Luke's time, and we didn't want that to be overshadowed by the sideshow of a highly visible dad. I finally decided that this was a great opportunity for the family to do something together. *This is your life now,* I thought. *Taking care of your family.* Surely the best way to do that was to be involved in the same world.

So the decision was made. Such a chance could come only once. It would be Luke's junior year, and if my part didn't go well, I could step away for his senior year.

The 2001 season was successful. My role was basically to serve as a consultant, backing up the young offensive coordinator, Jason Guthrie, and helping where I could. We made it as far as the initial rounds of the state playoffs. The great highlight was a trip to Florida to play another school at Disney World. You could see and feel our team bonding there, and for me it was a unique experience of being along for the ride on one of my kids' school events—a real rarity in my career. But someone in the media picked up on the story of this fired Tampa Bay coach coming back to central Florida with a high school team. They loved the story and covered it in the local news. For me it was an opportunity to tell the world I had no bitterness against anybody associated with the Buccaneers. My message was that I was the most fortunate of men. I had been given the opportunity to coach in the NFL, then coach my own son at the high school level. How many people ever get to do that?

But in the middle of the season, bad news came. My father went into the hospital for serious cancer surgery. At his bedside, my mother had a stroke. Both of them were in intensive care at the same time, but who would come to look after them? My sister, Aleita, couldn't be there because she was at home with two small children three thousand miles away in Portland, Oregon. She'd enjoyed a highly successful career as a television director and producer in Minneapolis and Portland, and she had been the director of my TV show when I was the head coach of the Minnesota Vikings. She had made the decision to step back from her career to be a full-time mom. With her husband traveling most weeks with his job, she had no choice but to stay at home with her kids.

My brother, Dave, was an assistant coach at the University of Missouri, and he was in the middle of his own football season. But as a volunteer coach, I had the freedom to simply take off and care for my parents for an extended period of time.

I realized once again that God knows the events we don't expect, and he has a plan. I had said this was a time for family—and it turned out to be so on multiple levels. My dad lived less than a year after his surgery, and we had a wonderful opportunity to say good-bye. If I'd been with an NFL team, that opportunity never would have come.

Fathers and Sons

After the 2001 season, Jack Daniels accepted an athletic director's position at Ravenwood, a new high school across town. Brentwood approached me about replacing him as head coach. But I told them I couldn't make that kind of commitment. As much as I enjoyed working with the kids at Brentwood, I knew that after Luke graduated I was likely to return to the NFL. Still, I made it clear that I'd love to remain on a volunteer basis.

Ron Crawford, the defensive coordinator from state champion Riverdale, became the new Brentwood coach. Ron is a great guy, and the kids loved playing for him. I was happy to find that he was comfortable keeping me around, and now he asked me to introduce and coordinate a new offense. "Given your background, we can all learn from you," he told me. "I know Jason welcomes your lead."

He also invited another volunteer with strong credentials: his own father, Tom Crawford, who had coached high school ball for many years.

Consequently, the Brentwood Bruins took on a kind of theme: father and son. There were the two Crawfords, the two Steckels—and one other interesting combo. Mike Jones was a former Titans player whom I knew well. He was yet another volunteer coach, a fellow with a heart more than big enough for his massive frame. One day some of the Titans had been approached by a young woman from the team's community relations office about a need for oversized clothing and shoes. It seemed there was a youngster named Steven whose mother was ill and unable to care for him. Steven was very tall for his age (eventually six feet six) and had huge feet. The young woman had thought perhaps some of the Titans had some extra stuff they could share. Mike and his wife, Javonda, immediately wanted to help, but they requested the opportunity to deliver the clothing personally.

When the Joneses met Steven, they fell in love with him. Here was a gentle, friendly kid who needed a break, and perhaps a male role model. Mike and Steven began to spend more time together. By the time his mother passed away, she had made the Joneses guardians of her son. They adopted Steven, even though they had small children of their own. Steven was not a football player, but with the help of Mike Jones, he became one very quickly. He came out for practice with his new adoptive dad and later received a football scholarship from the University of Tennessee.

I looked over the Bruins' roster and saw one remarkable story after another. For example, we had another player who had recently lost a parent. David Reed, a quiet young man who played tight end and defensive end, didn't say a lot off the field. But he worked hard at football. One day just before two-a-day practices began, his father was riding a tractor on his property when it overturned and killed him. It was a terrible shock for David and for the whole team. Coaches and players attended the funeral and gathered around to support David. My heart went out to this fatherless teenager. Several games into the season, David was scheduled to have his Eagle Scout ceremony, a very high honor. David asked me to stand up with him in the place where his dad would have been and to say a few words. It was a very moving and meaningful event for me, and one more reminder from God that this time would turn out to be about family in a deeper sense than I could have anticipated.

Then there was Glaydon Lifsey, a running back and one of Luke's best friends. He was unfortunate enough to have suffered a knee injury (a torn ACL) during his sophomore year. He returned for football as a junior even with the inconvenience of a knee brace. During his senior year he was still wearing that brace, but he tweaked the knee during the preseason. Glaydon was a fighter. There was no way to keep him from playing football. As the season progressed, the knee gave him more and more trouble, yet he rushed for over a thousand yards. Our playoff game against Hunters Lane would be his final performance on a gridiron. He made a leaping catch in the end zone and heard a pop in his knee as he came down with the ball. Glaydon had re-torn the same ACL.

Several painful surgeries followed. Glaydon's toughness and endurance were a symbol of that Brentwood Bruin football team—a group of young men that would never stop fighting regardless of the obstacles. Our senior leadership was strong and committed to one another. Matt "Whopper" Conner and Kevin Hartley led the offensive line—the men in the trenches. Austen Everson, our versatile quarterback, was our offensive captain. Our son Luke was the defensive captain and played middle linebacker. Joining him on defense were hard-hitting seniors: Rick Montgomery, Michael Clarke, and Parker Woodard. There were no Parade All-American or USA Today Top 100 blue-chip recruits on our team. But there was a roster filled with young men of character who squeezed every drop of achievement out of the talent God had given them.

I knew Luke had extra motivation during the 2002 season. He wanted to win for many reasons: because it was his senior year; because God had brought him back to the school he loved; because it meant something to play for his dad; because of the amazing group of young men who were his teammates; because he wanted to get it done for Glaydon; and because Luke believed something great was about to happen.

He would soon be proven right.

Everyone Involved

The Brentwood kids knew they were surrounded by schools with better talent: Riverdale in nearby Murfreesboro and Brentwood Academy right down the road, to name a couple. In its entire history, Brentwood had never made it further than the state quarterfinals. But there was an inner core, composed particularly of senior leaders, who believed they could achieve something special. They pushed themselves in the weight room during the off-season with a sign in front of them telling how many days remained until the state championship. Each day they marked off another number and kept their eyes on the prize.

I admired their youthful ambition, but for years it had been my business to evaluate football talent. I knew what Brentwood had and what some of the other schools had. Just making it deeper into the playoffs would be a nice achievement for this bunch. State championship? Well, it was sound motivation. But never tell young people what they cannot do—particularly when they're high in the character category.

I also enjoyed mentoring one of the young coaches. Two or three times a week, Jason Guthrie would come to our home and I would teach him the intricacies of the offense I was putting in. Chris would make lunch, and we'd eat and talk Xs and Os. Jason was an eager learner, a team player with a great attitude, like everyone associated with the Brentwood Bruins that year.

The kids wanted to do something special in 2002, so the coaches held practice accordingly. Preseason camp was another grueling boot camp environment. We pushed the kids hard, and some of them were talking about quitting. Coach Crawford and I told them, "Hang in there. Stick it out, and you'll get your chance to play." I brought in the strategy I had used at Brown University years ago, with multiple personnel groupings. Everyone had a role. For example, there was a track athlete who could really run. We had plays that simply required him to sprint toward the end zone. We might not throw to him, but he would clear out a defensive back that would help someone else get open. He was excited about having a role to play.

These groupings had colorful names based on their interests or roles—there was a NASCAR team, a TANK team, and a JET team. There was a team called BASEBALL, made up of five skilled players who were actually on the baseball team. We'd yell, "NASCAR!" and that group would run into the game. If you weren't part of the NASCAR group, you came off the field. This strategy allowed us to make use of a lot of players who ordinarily never would have gotten into a game. We might call for them only once or twice, but they knew their role, they practiced it repeatedly, and they got it done par excellence when the time came. The personnel groups built morale. They built unity. Up and down the bench our players were alert for every minute of regulation, waiting to hear their group name called. Everyone stayed involved and therefore motivated. I believe that's a significant key to the success of any organization—allowing everyone to use their strengths and make a contribution.

Getting all the kids involved was only part of the equation. We worked hard to get the families involved as well. Our games were on Friday nights, of course. The rest of the weekend was for rest, then Monday we reviewed the game and had a light workout. On Tuesday afternoons we focused on the defense, and Wednesday was all about the offense. So we asked the parents for a big favor. "On Tuesdays after practice," we asked, "would you come in and serve us a big homemade dinner for the offensive players so we can stay and discuss the week's game plan?"

Those moms and dads grabbed the idea and ran with it. Groups of three or four mothers took turns fixing terrific potluck feasts, and we fed the offense in a large classroom in the school. The players would come in after practice and their eyes would grow wide. They'd say, "Wow!" when they saw all the food. We would enjoy dinner together, then I'd get up in front of the chalkboard and begin to lay out the game plan. The kids would listen carefully, then practice their assignments the next day. We also had Thursday night dinners for seniors in their homes. We realized that just as the kids competed on the practice field, we had the mothers competing to out-cook each other! Everybody was a winner, because we had some fantastic dinners.

Other than good eating, why were these gatherings a good idea? Because families were drawn together. Older teenagers are beginning to be more independent and may start to drift away from their parents. We found a way to pull everyone together in a way that would create a family memory even as we were getting our training and planning done—not to mention the bonding of teammates. Parents were accustomed to sitting in the stands; they loved being part of the team and making a contribution.

We survived the preseason two-a-day workouts. We put the personnel groups together. And we got the dinner idea off the ground. We could feel our team coming together.

Now all we had to do was play the games.

Teeing It Up

There's never a problem motivating players for Game One. By that time they're tired of pounding on each other in practice, and they're hungry for a live opponent. But our first adversary really stood out: Brentwood Academy, the private school less than a mile away.

There was a natural community rivalry between these local private and public schools, but for our guys the incentive cut even deeper. We had lost only one game during the previous regular season: to Brentwood Academy in the opening game. The academy brought in scholarship players, and was often ranked in USA Today's Top Twenty.

The Battle of Brentwood came on a hot, humid evening in late August—over ninety degrees at game time. It was a hard-fought battle from the opening drive to the closing moments, when our last drive to take the lead came up short. We lost the game, and our players were devastated. They had pointed to a state championship but particularly to the jump–start that would come from revenge over a rival. For months their whole focus had been on this game.

Yet for the second straight year, we were 0–1. The goal of an unde-feated season was already beyond us. I felt terrible about the dejec-tion of our players. I felt disappointed in my game plan. One thing I discovered was that I was basing the timing of my plays on a faster game. High school football moved much slower than the NFL, so the timing was off. I would have to acclimate myself to the slower play development to synchronize our offense.

The game had been over for an hour when Luke and a few of his friends emerged from the field house and strolled back onto the empty field. The big lights were still lit, but the stadium was empty and quiet. So were the boys at first. They walked around and began to share their frustration and disappointment. Each one thought he could have played better and thought the guys simply didn't execute their assignments.

Then Luke challenged the mood. He said, "It hurts bad to lose. We know we can play better and that we didn't get it done. But I'll tell you what: after nine months without football, it felt good to put on the pads tonight. I had fun just playing."

His friends quickly voiced their agreement. It was bad to lose but good to play. The guys stood around the field for half an hour talk-ing about football and how much they loved it. And they began to feel better by degrees, and to be sure, they didn't lose any of their edge. The Bruins weren't finished; they were only starting. It's a cliché, but there was a lot of football left to be played. After all, the game that night was an out-of-conference game; in a way, it didn't even count. The magic was still possible.

I think some of the stars fell out of our players' eyes that night. They became tougher and more realistic. The goals were still the goals, but they lacked the superhuman ability to cruise to easy victo-ries. It was going to take hard work to get beyond this defeat and become the team they knew they could be.

Comeback

For me, it felt good to settle into the rhythm of a football season. Chris and I would pick up doughnuts or bagels and watch game film with the coaches on Saturday mornings. On Sundays after church, I didn't even think of turning on the TV to see what was happening in that other universe called the NFL. I was totally immersed in the world of Brentwood High School football. I'd create a game plan, Chris would type it out, and by Tuesday night the offense had it in hand. So Luke, Chris, and I were living the football life as a family, and we were having fun.

People often ask what it was like to coach high school after the NFL, particularly as a volunteer. They figure it must have been a piece of cake. I tell them it was the most pressure I ever felt in thirty-two years of coaching. For one thing, we were starting to win consistently, and we were hearing people say, "Oh, we'll win the state because we have NFL coaching!" It's not so easy, of course. It's one thing to deal with owners, general managers, and the press. It's another thing for me to feel that I could disappoint friends and parents of teenagers I was coming to know and love. The last thing I wanted to do was let them down. We loved the people so much: the kids, their parents, and the coaches. So I felt the pressure, but it was the kind of pressure you can thrive under.

As the season wore on, it seemed as if it was always raining on Friday night. All kinds of storms were moving through the Southeast that autumn. Yet the team was beginning to shine through the clouds.

Game Four was against Centennial, a fairly new school in the county. They had never beaten Brentwood at any level of football: freshman, junior varsity, or varsity. So those guys circled the game on their schedule the way we circled Brentwood Academy. Centennial came in breathing fire, highly motivated to knock us off.

As usual, the rain was coming down. The Brentwood field was muddy, and our team was uninspired. This was a game Brentwood was accustomed to winning. Our guys lacked the emotional charge they would bring to a huge game. As we moved deeper into the second half, we knew we were in trouble. We were ahead, but Centennial was driving in the final moments. Our quarterback, Austen, was one of Luke's closest friends and probably the best athlete on the team. He's your basic all-American boy and "homecoming king," but underneath all that he's one tough football player with great Christian character. We inserted him in the game as a defensive back to defend against the pass. But Centennial quickly threw a touchdown pass over Austen's head. Austen was devastated. He thought he had lost the game for his team.

With one minute left on the clock, Glaydon Lifsey fielded the ensuing kickoff and made a spectacular run, slashing through the kickoff coverage and returning the ball to midfield. Austen stepped into the huddle, looked his teammates in the eye, and said, "Okay, guys. I got us into this mess, and I'm going to get us out of it."

I thought about calling a double reverse pass. Austen, the quarterback, would hand the ball off to Glaydon deep in the backfield. As Glaydon ran to his right, Luke (who played H-back on offense) would run toward him from his splitout position to take a second handoff on the reverse. Moving left as a left-hander, Luke could easily pass the ball to Austen streaking down the left sideline. No one on defense would be assigned to cover the quarterback in Centennial's man-to-man coverage, so he should be wide open. This would be quite a play call for rain, mud, and high school kids. Sitting in the press box, I may have worried more about that call than any I made on national television in a professional game. I loved those kids and didn't want them to be crushed by an upset loss.

I sent the play down anyway. When the signal came in, Austen's eyes grew wide. Glaydon and Luke just looked at each other, as if to say,

"What is Coach Steckel thinking?" But the play worked. So did another big clutch pass play that put us inside the 5, with eleven ticks on the clock. And that clock was still running, ten seconds, nine, eight . . .

But our guys were unflappable; they knew what to do. Austen started yelling, "Geronimo! Geronimo!" Remember that Buffalo playoff game? This was that same no-huddle play. Centennial players thought the game was ending as we ran a play directly into the line and got stuffed. But our guys jumped to their feet, quickly came set at the line, and snapped the ball, catching our opponent off guard. Austen faked the halfback dive and sprinted around the end for a touchdown. The crowd exploded. Brentwood had a huge, character-building, come-from-behind victory.

Chris and I walked into the parking lot after the game. The wetness was dampening none of our kids' spirits. Everyone was hooping and hollering and celebrating. But after the crowd was gone, Chris and I sat in our car and prayed. We thanked God for providing such a wonderful, joyful experience for these young men, the coaches, and the students who loved the team. We thanked him for bringing us to this community and letting us be a part of something so meaningful. We thanked him that whatever happens in life, his plan is always wiser and more wonderful than we can imagine.

Into the Playoffs

The Centennial game was a turning point for our team. The guys began to see themselves as overcomers—as one unified band of brothers that could find a way to win. If they could get it done when they didn't bring their best game; if they could get it done against an inspired opponent and inclement weather; if they could get it done even with Les Steckel's insane play-calling—who knew what might be possible? The kids began to believe.

From there we started winning each week almost methodically. We won the close ones, and we won a few that were not so close. And suddenly, there we were facing the playoffs. Just as in the preceding season, we had run the table after losing our opener to Brentwood Academy. But what now? Were we going to repeat the script by bowing out of the playoffs early? This team had never won a state championship. It had never gotten beyond the quarterfinals. How could we knock the lid off the program and go to the next level?

I was almost ready to leave the house for our playoff game against neighboring Franklin, another big rival, when the doorbell rang. Our son C.T. was standing there with a big grin on his face, having flown all the way from Los Angeles to see his little brother play football. He went the distance to support the brother he loved. His mother, of course, had no idea he was coming and had already left to save seats at the stadium. After C.T. and I arrived there, I could hear Chris's shout of surprise all the way up in the press box when he appeared at her side in the stands.

C.T. told his mother, "Don't let Luke know I'm here. I don't want any more pressure on him or anything."

Chris said, "Are you kidding? You get down there right now, and after pregame warm-up, you let him know you're here, how much you love him, and wish him good luck."

C.T. wasn't sure. He said, "You think that would be better?"

A chorus of mothers broke in, agreeing with Chris: "Absolutely!" "Oh yes!" "That's what I would do."

As C.T. bowed to the will of the majority, from my high perch I watched my two sons sharing a hug. I realized again that I was enjoying something no Super Bowl could match.

The game itself lived up to its setup. The place was packed, people were sitting on the adjoining hills and all around the running track, and you couldn't have fit in another fan with a shoehorn. The teams exchanged touchdowns and leads. At the end, we were clinging to a five-point advantage, and Franklin was driving for the victory. They were down to our 20-yard line with twenty-three seconds left, and there was incredible tension. The Franklin quarterback dropped back to pass and hurled a missile toward the goal line as our hearts stopped.

The pass never got there. Luke, dropping deep into the end zone, snatched it out of the air, locked it away, and thus punched our ticket to the state semifinals—a world Brentwood High had never explored. Luke's interception was athletic—an extended, two-handed leap that was like a dive off the high board. The players danced on the field, and I felt like dancing myself. Tonight we had proven we were something special.

Only one more team was standing between us and the big game. But what a team it was: Germantown, on the far end of the state, a perennial power in the Memphis area.

Our players had talked about practicing on Thanksgiving morning as a team goal. In their minds, working on a holiday symbolized their commitment and determination. It was bitterly cold and windy, but we had a great, brisk practice.

The challenge of the playoffs is that each week the stakes are higher. Each week the opponent is tougher and more talented, the weather is colder, and your players are wearier and more beaten up. The further you go, the greater the challenge and the more it's going to hurt when you finally take the fall. But you accept all of that and gladly, because going deep into the playoffs is a thing that might come along once in a lifetime. Win it all, and you have a story for your grandchildren.

Germantown was the obstacle blocking our path. They had been the top-ranked team in the state from week one until now. To make things more difficult, we had to climb into the bus and ride for hours to play at their place. Yet somehow halftime arrived and we had a nice lead. I was in shock. The players piled into the locker room saying to each other, "One more half! One more half, and we play for it *all*." They were already getting themselves pumped about *next* week.

But Luke had been around a few teams, a few coaching staffs, and a few situations like this one. He said, "Get ready, guys. Here come the coaches."

Sure enough, we quickly stuffed a cork into any premature celebrations. "Take those smiles off your faces! You think this is a big deal, guys?" we said. "This is halftime. You know how many points those guys can score in the second half? You haven't won anything yet." Relaxing is the quickest way to lose a lead and a game.

The second half tightened up, just as we predicted. Germantown came out of the locker room and drove quickly downfield for a touchdown to make the score 21–7. Later, an interception and touchdown return made our lead too close for comfort. We drove the ball down the field behind the running of Jared Fugate, our junior running back, and a determined offensive line to get us a game-clinching field goal with three minutes remaining. We held on and won 24–14, and the ride home was a very happy one. We were on our way to the state championship.

When we got back to our home, we found it decorated with a colorful banner all the way across the front. Balloons were everywhere. Mike Munchak, my coaching friend from the Titans who lived across the street, had done the decorating with his wife, Marci, and their daughters, Alex and Julie—great friends, great neighbors.

Another friend was also excited. Ed Rush came all the way from Phoenix, Arizona. He had been following the season and the playoffs over the Internet. He had claimed that if we played in the championship game, he would buy an airline ticket and join us at the "Big Dance." Ed made good on his promise, and visiting with him during championship week added another layer of pleasure to the festivities.

Who would be our opponent? Riverdale—our head coach's old team and the reigning state champs; a Tennessee high school dynasty. It was Riverdale's fifth state championship game in eight years, and they had won it three times. You couldn't have scripted it better in Hollywood. Coach Crawford, in his first year away from Riverdale, was coming home to challenge his good friend Head Coach Gary Rankin.

For All the Marbles

Try to imagine the pressure. This was the state championship, and for our kids, Riverdale was the ultimate opponent. It was old news for Riverdale to play for the trophy, but not for us. There was a great deal of publicity, especially for a high school game. Our kids were crazy with excitement. Their parents may have been even crazier. The local NBC affiliate sent cameras to film me working on my game plan, Luke preparing to leave for the game, and all of us getting ready. Then they wanted to film me in the press box calling plays. I was more nervous than I had ever been in any football game, Super Bowls included. This one was for the kids. This one was for the family.

We managed a touchdown in the second quarter on a beautiful 80-yard drive, and we had the lead. But then a terrible thing happened. On the extra point, our kicker, Kyle Willis, took a brutal hit and severly injured his ankle. The bigger a game is, the more important is the kicking game—and we had lost our team's Big Toe. Safety Michael Clarke had to step up for us as the backup kicker.

The game was incredibly tight. Our lead was threatened right before halftime when Riverdale reached our 14. But our linebacker Ian Van Horne sacked the Riverdale quarterback, and time ran out before he could spike the ball to stop the clock. Riverdale had been in the shadow of our end zone without scoring. We had dodged a bullet.

In the fourth quarter, somehow we still had a shutout and a chance to practically ice the game. Our defense came through once again, just as they so often did throughout the season, with a huge interception. We were driving for our second score, managing the clock, when we found ourselves at second down inside the 20. It was here that I made a conservative call. We called time-out, and I asked Coach Crawford to put our quarterback on the headphones. I said, "Austen, I want you take the snap, give it to Jared, and tell him to run the ball to the left, over to the very center of the field between the hash-marks. We're going to bring in Michael to kick a field goal, and we need the ball in the middle of the field." In other words, I was playing for the field goal and a two-score lead late in the game.

Three points would be huge for us in this situation. But it was a tremendous risk, because we didn't know if our backup kicker could come through under this kind of pressure. Austen and Jared carried out their assignments so that Michael had a straight shot at the cross-bar. Then Michael nailed the kick, and we had a 10–0 lead in the fourth quarter. I couldn't help but feel very good and very proud of these young men. We had the reigning champions down by ten in their hometown in the fourth quarter. Could we hang on? Riverdale had the ability to score quickly.

Our defense got a big stop, and Riverdale punted us deep into our own territory. After two consecutive short runs, we were forced into a third and long situation. On third down, I called a short side-line pass. I felt that we had to get a first down and keep possession of the ball. The last thing I wanted to do was give Riverdale the ball back. Austen rolled to his right and drilled the ball to one of our wide receivers. It bounced off his chest and into the hands of a Riverdale defensive back. The Riverdale sideline erupted. To make things worse, a penalty was tacked on after the return. Moments later, a touchdown tightened the game to 10–7. The momentum had completely changed.

The ensuing kickoff placed us in a dangerous place, deep in our own territory. I called two running plays to eat up as much time as possible. We wanted the clock to tick away, but the time just didn't seem to move fast enough. Our running game had grounded out some tough yards, but that critical third down was staring us in the face again. Soon we would be looking at a punt that would give them good field position. And our defense had to be tiring.

Then I looked down on the field and saw it. Riverdale had gone into a defensive alignment I had been looking for all season.

I had scripted a play called a "whip route" for Kellen Moore, one of our wide receivers. All year we practiced it, and Kellen ran it as well as anyone I'd coached in the NFL. But it was dictated by a certain defensive coverage that we never saw. Now, right in the fourth quarter of the state championship game, Riverdale was using the tight man-to-man coverage ready-made for the whip route.

But here we were again, in the same part of the field where we had just thrown a very costly interception. I had just helped demonstrate the high risk of putting the ball in the air in this kind of situation. It ran against all known football logic, especially for a championship game. If the ball was picked off, or if we fumbled or were sacked, I might be inducted into the Bonehead Hall of Fame.

But I knew it was there. I decided to make the call.

Austen dropped back in the pocket. Kellen ran inside, then whipped back out, and Austen threw the ball. Kellen was wide open and made the catch for the first down, and the Riverdale defensive back missed the tackle. Kellen was working his way down the field, and I was saying to myself, "*Down*, Kellen—just fall down!" I was terrified that he might fumble the ball. But he went down safely. We were out of the danger zone with two minutes remaining.

Mike Heimerdinger, who succeeded me as the Titans' offensive coordinator, had a son named Brian on our team. Mike told me after the game, "Les, I can't believe the —— you had to call that whip route!" As two NFL offensive play-callers, we had a great laugh about it.

We bled the clock with three running plays, but with time running out we had to punt. Once again the pressure was on Michael Clarke, who coolly nailed a 41-yard punt that pinned Riverdale back on their own 10. But our opponent mounted a furious rally back to the 50. Our defense was tired, and our opponent was coming to life, making their big play to keep us from stealing their championship. Everyone on our side was hoping and praying that we could do it one more time: step up, stop Riverdale, win the game. Fourteen seconds remained. Riverdale didn't need a touchdown. They only needed to get into field goal range. Three points would tie the game and send it into overtime.

The Riverdale quarterback faded back to pass. Our defensive ends were bearing down on him, and the quarterback stepped to one side and rifled the ball down the middle of the field. Our hearts stopped. Suddenly a blue jersey appeared. It was number 9, snagging the ball and falling backward.

It was Luke Steckel.

You couldn't have heard a jetliner landing at midfield. Everyone on the Brentwood side was screaming. Luke slid back on the turf, clutching the football for dear life, then dropped forward to his knees and pointed to the sky, to heaven, to God; to the God who had once angered him by moving him away from this school and these friends. Luke understood now.

In that one moment, there was an incredible synchronicity to everything in my life and the life of my family. All of it came together: struggling with the Vikings, fighting through brokenness and firings, Super Bowls and college bowls and too many moving vans. I could almost feel the hand of the Lord on my shoulder, and I knew what he would be saying to me: *Here it is, Les. All of those years of searching for your heart's desire, from Bloomington to Boulder, from Tennessee to Tampa— here is what you were searching for. Here is the joy I've wanted to give you. Look at the hands of your son.*

Luke was being mobbed by his teammates. But I knew what was on his hands. On one wristband he had taken a marker and scrawled 2 CHRON 15:7, which reads, "But as for you, be strong and do not give up, for your work will be rewarded" (NIV). On his other wristband he had written "Pop-Pop." That was the name he used for his granddad—my father, who didn't live to see this victory.

Those wristbands carried his personal motivation as well as the story of my life—faith on one hand, family on the other; and together those two hands cradled a football, the medium by which God has taught me so many things. I felt a supreme joy at that moment, not about winning a game but about serving a God who is so gracious and loving, so wise and foresighted. It was one of those rare moments when God seems to roll back the curtain and show us the life and the love he had in mind all along—a life in which all the pain and sacrifice find their redemption in the warmth of his grace.

The Gang's All Here

Earlier in the season a message was left on our phone by Tony Dungy in Indianapolis. By this time Tony had been fired at Tampa Bay and taken the Indianapolis Colts job. In his message he said, "Les, I want you to know that I've been thinking about you and your family. I pray for you and your family every Friday, though I don't know what specifics to pray about. I wanted to tell you I was doing this because God put it on my heart to pray for you on that day of the week."

I had a big smile when I called Tony back. "Hey, Tony," I said. "Thanks for leaving that message. And guess what? I'm coaching a high school team, and we play when you pray—on Fridays. We're winning every game. So you keep praying, and we'll keep playing—it works!"

He laughed. "Really? That's great."

"As a matter of fact, we're heading for the semifinals and hopefully the finals after that."

Tony thought that was outstanding, and he called on a Saturday to see if we were still alive in the playoff tournament. I told him we were getting ready for the state championship game and that the big game was coming on the following Saturday.

He said, "You're kidding me."

"Not at all," I said. "As a matter of fact, your Colts will be right here in town to play the Titans on the following day. On Saturday you'll be sitting in your hotel room, and you can watch the Brentwood Bruins play on your TV."

Tony could hardly believe it.

Sometimes when these amazing moments come, God just seems to wrap them up in a nice package with his signature written plainly on the tag. That championship weekend was one of those moments. On Saturday we had our victory; on Sunday I was on the field with a sideline pass for the Titans-Colts game in the Adelphia Coliseum. During the pregame warm-up, I saw Tony Dungy, and we had a great time together. Then I grabbed Jeff Fisher and gave him a big hug. Old Titan friends—coaches and players—were there too. It felt to me like *This Is Your Life, Les Steckel*—a reunion of all the key players from my recent adventures.

I was able to watch the game from the sidelines and take in all the flavor of the NFL strictly as an observer. I said a little prayer then: "God, thank you for giving me the privilege of being part of this pro football world, now and tomorrow. But thank you also for letting me find the deeper joy of helping to coach my own son, and the sons of some terrific families, to a high school championship. There is nothing on earth I would trade for that experience. Thanks also, Lord, for so many other blessings: David Reed's Eagle Scout ceremony; time with my dad before he passed away; more time with Chris and our three children; the joy of seeing my kids' love for each other; knowing Mike and Steven Jones; friendship with the other Brentwood coaches; bringing me together with Tony Dungy and Jeff Fisher today. Who could orchestrate such things but you? Your hand is unmistakable, Lord. And your plan is so much better, so much richer, so much more joyful than any game plan I ever could have drawn up."

That was one of the greatest days of my life. And somehow, I knew the best was yet to come. I knew even then that tomorrow was bound to hold even greater surprises and richer lessons. That's just the way it is with the kind of God we serve. As the apostle Paul put it, "I keep working toward that day when I will finally be all that Christ Jesus saved me for and wants me to be" (Phil. 3:12).

That, my friend, is the most rewarding work in this world.

The Extra Point

Coaches have come up to me several times with the same comment: "Les, you're the luckiest guy in the world. You get to coach in the Super Bowl, then you get to coach your own son to a state championship."

I can't argue, except for the use of the word *lucky*. I would substitute another word: *blessed*.

The difference is in realizing that God really does have a plan. This life has its challenging moments, but I hope you've learned in this book that those who follow God have the opportunity to turn their defeats into victories.

What a journey it has been to relive my life in this book. I've been humbled to realize just how often the hand of God was at work in my life when I didn't even realize it. More than ever I know that he uses all things for our good (Rom. 8:28). More than ever I'm confident that when life knocks me down at some point in the future, I'll be able to fight on with the knowledge that hardships are just raw material for another part of God's amazing plan—the plan that always provides me with a future and a hope.

Have you ever spent a short time revisiting your own journey? Where can you see the handiwork of your Creator, who loves you, helping you toward a blessing you never could have anticipated? What new adventure might he be setting up in your life right now?

Take some time today to do some big-picture thinking about your own life. Try these questions on for size:

- What was your last major setback? How did God use it? What did you learn?
- What is the greatest challenge you are facing in life right now?
- What great blessing do you think might be just around the corner for you?

Life can throw nothing at you that God can't use for your benefit. This is *your* life. It was carefully drawn up in God's playbook just for you. If you totally trust him, he won't let your life end one yard short.

11

After Further Review

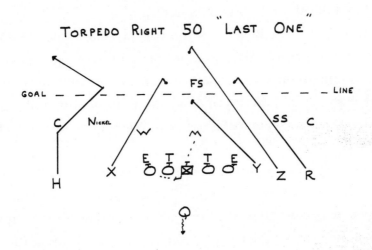

TORPEDO RIGHT 50 "LAST ONE"

One more coaching opportunity came my way: a year with the Buffalo Bills. I was reunited with former Titans Coach Gregg Williams, who was then the head coach of the Bills. I coached running backs that year and had the opportunity to build relationships with some terrific men.

The Bills won only six games, and most of the staff was dismissed at the end of the year. By this time in my career, that was nothing new. I had learned to roll with the punches and keep trusting God. We made some good friends at our church in Buffalo and never regretted the time we had there.

At the same time, Chris and I were keeping busier than ever with speaking engagements. We really enjoy traveling together and sharing with audiences about marriage and coaching.

We did a lot of work for FCA as well. That organization has been a constant in my career, ever since that first convention in 1972 in Hollywood, Florida, when I was checking out the coaching profession. I remember walking along in the hotel lobby and seeing a large banner reading "Fellowship of Christian Athletes." I thought, *Now what could that be all about?* An impressive gentleman named Bruce Bickel told me about FCA and its ministry.

It turned out that Bruce was the backup quarterback for Roger Staubach at the Naval Academy, and naturally that was a detail that caught my attention. I was a Staubach fan anyway, and my dream had once been to attend the Naval Academy. On top of that, Bruce had served in Vietnam as a navy fighter pilot. Needless to say, we had a lot of mutual interests.

Bruce sparked my interest in this organization called FCA. I learned how it all started back in 1954 as a result of the vision of a young man named Don McClanen, who collected press clippings about professional athletes who spoke out about their Christian faith. Before anyone else, Don saw an opportunity for evangelism in a modern context—heroes of athletics could become heroes of the faith. Don began to contact people like Carl Erskine, Otto Graham, Donn Moomaw, and Branch Rickey.

FCA was only in its second decade when I met Bruce Bickel in Hollywood, Florida. Over the years I was able to grow along with the ministry and see many other coaches and players become stronger in their faith and bear spiritual fruit, all from the context of professional sports.

For example, Dal Shealy, the recently retired former president of FCA, recalls the time when he was a young high school coach and saw a sign for a free FCA breakfast at a meeting of the American Football Coaches Association. "I didn't understand anything about

FCA, but I understood 'breakfast' and 'free,' " he has told us. The next thing he knew, he was at an FCA Camp learning how to grow in his faith. He became head football coach at the University of Richmond before devoting his career fully to FCA.

That's just one story among thousands, including that of my family. Over the years, Chris and I became more and more involved with this influential ministry, and it has had so many positive influences in our lives. Chris loves to kid me about the fact that she became a national board member of FCA before I did. When we were in Tampa, FCA President Dal Shealy asked her to come onto the board. I couldn't believe it! Receiving such an appointment was a dream of mine. So when she told me about her new honor, I blurted out, "They asked you and not *me*?"

"Don't worry. Once I'm on, I'll put in a good word for you," Chris teased me.

Eventually we both were on the board of FCA and committed to its goals.

On to Ministry

In 2004 Chris and I were in Kansas City for the fiftieth anniversary celebration of FCA. It was great to see all our friends from across the years, from camps, coaches' retreats, rallies, and other events in which we had worked together. One evening I was in the hallway of our hotel when Grant Teaff walked up and said hello. Grant, who had been a very successful football coach at Baylor University and serves as the executive director of the American Football Coaches Association, is a dynamic personality who is deeply involved with FCA. Dal was retiring as president of the ministry, and Grant was involved in finding a replacement. He asked me if I was willing to interview for that position. His interest humbled me.

It was something to think about. Since the time I was a young marine, I had worn a coach's whistle, stood on sidelines, and sat in press boxes. Being in full-time ministry would be quite a transition, so I had to pray and seek God's will for my life very carefully. I certainly still enjoyed coaching and had opportunities to stay in the NFL doing what I'd always done.

As I engaged in a series of interviews, the primary question the committee asked was, "Are you able to walk away from coaching?" It was a good question, and I felt powerful emotions upon hearing it. I couldn't speak for a few moments. It has been said, "Once a coach, always a coach." Working with young athletes seemed to be the way God wired me. It brought me joy. Could an old dog learn a few new tricks?

A few days beforehand I had asked God to speak to me about my future. During that time of prayer, he had led me to Luke 5:10, in which Jesus says, "Don't be afraid! From now on you'll be fishing for people!" What a significant prophecy that verse now seems to provide.

After a season of seeking God's will, I had an answer for the committee's question. "I think I could join this team," I said. "Team FCA." I realized that I wouldn't be giving up coaching after all, just taking it to a new level. I understood that all my past was prelude—every coaching experience had prepared me for this one. The lure of living from Sunday to Sunday for wins and losses began to fade as I envisioned this new challenge in the business of life and death.

For some time I had felt God preparing me for something new. So much had happened leading up to the wonderful experience of helping the Brentwood Bruins win a state championship. My values were changing. For years my life had been all about offenses and defenses, Xs and Os. But I was drawn more and more to the greater issues of life. During our time in Brentwood, we'd had a wonderful experience at Brentwood Baptist Church. I had served on the staff as "coach in residence" and led two very popular Bible studies for men, Tuesday Morning Quarterback Club and Top Gun.

Those experiences were teaching me that people today are hungry to integrate their spiritual lives with their careers and their families. They need guidance and encouragement. I looked out at all those faces, and somehow they reminded me of the old gymnasiums where I had learned the skill of boxing, back at Kansas University. I often saw the faces of men on the ropes in the fourteenth round. Many of them were bone-weary, bruised, struggling to stay on their feet and avoid the knockdown. They would come in on these Tuesday mornings, and I would become the trainer in their corner, wiping away the sweat and encouraging them to go one more round. Those Bible study groups attracted men from every direction, and I could feel that God was beginning to use me in a new way. Those men meant a lot to me—more than they'll ever know.

New World, New Goals

I decided some time ago that I wanted the second half of my life to center on significance. What an amazing opportunity Chris and I have been given to attain that goal.

We live in a sports-crazy society where athletes have the chance to be role models and tone-setters. I look at the world of professional sports, where I've spent so many years, and I see that today it's out of bounds. There's too much *me* and not enough *we* in sports; too much showmanship and not enough sportsmanship. FCA is hard at work becoming the heart and soul in sports. We want to put Christian character back between the lines. In our vision to see the world impacted for Jesus Christ through athletes and coaches, we emphasize four Cs: Coaches, Campus, Camps, and Community. It's our game plan to fulfill the vision we have for bringing spiritual revival to our culture.

- *Coaches.* Who in our society has a deeper influence on young people than their coaches? I think about the impact of Jesus Christ through FCA in my own life, in the lives of folks like Dal Shealy, Grant Teaff, and so many others. I think about the "ripple effect" of the influence of coaches on young people and their families. It gets my blood pumping to think of what could happen to this world if we could serve, minister to, and begin working alongside every single one of those coaches. It is said that one coach on one campus can influence over ten thousand lives in a career. Their impact for Christ could change generations to come.

- *Campus.* I wish I had time and space enough to write about everything happening on our campuses these days, but you're probably aware of it. Amid a world of tension and growing violence and danger for our young people, FCA provides more than a few rays of hope through our outstanding Huddle groups, team Bible studies, chapel programs, and *One Way to Play—Drug Free!* (our program to confront the problem of drug and alcohol abuse). Our Huddles enable young people to enhance and explore their faith in a way that can change their campuses from the inside out.

- *Camps.* As a young college coach, I had my way paid to my first FCA Camp by a wonderful fellow coach named Dan Stavely. What a significant event that was for me. Today more than thirty thousand athletes, coaches, and their families attend more than one hundred fifty FCA Camps across America each year. Devoted to introducing Christ to coaches and athletes through their passion for sports, FCA Camps provide life-changing experiences. A week of "inspiration and perspiration," our camps range from football to golf, from soccer to lacrosse, from motocross to surfing, and most sports in between. FCA Camps are great experiences where lives are changed one heart at a time.

- *Community.* FCA is deeply involved in service and ministry within our communities. The tremendous growth in club, league, and church sports has challenged FCA to reach out beyond the campus and camps. In partnership with local churches, businesses, parents, and volunteers, FCA has established many sports-specific ministries to reach athletes and coaches off campus as well.

The potential to influence lives for Christ through FCA is boundless. In other words, this is a work worth exchanging the rest of my life for—and that's all I have to give. Chris and I are heading into the second half of life with renewed passion. When I called plays in the Super Bowl, the whole world was watching. When we call our plays now, the whole world is *waiting*. We want every living soul to know God's truth. I wonder if, through reading this book, you feel God calling you to join our effort and help guarantee that no one falls one yard short of the eternal victory.

Super Bowl Reunion

I've been told, "Les, I hear you retired into that FCA job." Chris and I have a good laugh about that one! Retired? We're on the go more than ever. Chris and I are in a new city nearly every week, speaking, encouraging, and furthering the global ministry of FCA every way we can.

That's daily life for us. We move through the airport of the day, trying to keep up with our luggage and our three children, the latter through cell phones and occasional visits. You may recall that the last to leave our nest was Luke, who had such a memorable senior experience at Brentwood High School. He, too, had to figure out where to go next in life. We laughed when he jokingly asked, "Mom, Dad— what if my life has already peaked?"

We've learned enough to know better. As great as that championship season was, we know that God has miraculous surprises in store for all three of our children. But we did need to find Luke a college. While he ended up at Princeton, we visited several others together. One of those was the University of North Carolina at Chapel Hill.

UNC is a beautiful Southern campus. We enjoyed our trip, and the football coaches invited Luke to come see the athletic facilities. So we had a good visit with some of the coaches. Naturally, they knew I'd coached college and pro teams, so they asked me to speak to the staff. I stood in front of the chalkboard and talked a few Xs and Os with them. Eventually the subject came around to "the play"—I'll give you three guesses which one. It's on the cover of this book. I always expect that question.

So I diagrammed the play on the board and gave a clear explanation of why we called it, what we had learned about the defensive tendencies of the St. Louis Rams, and why we felt that play would give us the victory. What made the explanation a little different this time was that John Bunting was standing in the back of the room. John was the co-defensive coordinator for the St. Louis Rams in that very Super Bowl and was now the head coach at UNC. That famous play had pitted the two of us as coaching adversaries, and here we were for a reunion. In life, the ball takes funny bounces sometimes.

John listened politely to my explanation, nodding appreciatively at several points. Finally, he said, "They had us dead. They had us dead to rights. The play just came up one yard short."

So I called the play that seemed right, John agreed that it was the right call, but other variables came into play. Sometimes we never find out, in this life, what factors shaped our destiny. Other times we figure it out after further review.

Imagine the heaven that awaits you and me. I wonder if there's a film room up there, where we'll review the key plays of our lives. I can imagine standing in that room with those whose paths we crossed in life and watching the replays together. What will we learn after further review?

The Extra Point

On the evening of Super Bowl XXXIV, I felt that my play call had gone wrong. But from the film room in Chapel Hill, and from the other side of several pivotal years, I could see the exact same play as something else entirely. Only from a human perspective did it fail. From the eternal perspective, God used it to help redefine what my life was all about. It was no longer about wins and losses; it was about life and death. He asked me, *Do you know how many people out there are one yard short of eternal victory?* He meant the ultimate victory over the ultimate defeat.

I can also look at that play and realize that in my life it was not the Main Event but merely the prelude to one. All it did was sweeten the joy I experienced when a championship finally did materialize—a true adventure involving my family and people I'd come to love. Now I could understand.

In the film room of heaven, I know all my questions will finally be answered. I'll know just what the Master Coach was doing when he called this or that play. I'll know just where I zigged when I should have zagged; just how God bailed me out of even more mistakes than I realized—because his plan is perfect and he has never missed a single call.

I wonder what plays you'll see from your own life in that film room. What is God trying to accomplish through your life? What words is he trying to whisper in your ear?

My prayer for you is that his voice won't be lost in the roar of the crowd or the crunch of your daily life. I'm living proof that he has a plan for every single one of us and that no matter how hard we try, we're still incapable of envisioning how wonderful God's plan is, compared to the flawed and unsatisfying dreams we concoct for ourselves.

Believe me, I never imagined my life would be a book. But God gives each one of us a story, and God wants to help you write new chapters that will help you bring victory out of defeat.

So read the pages of your own life, my friend. Take one more look at the film. After further review, I think you'll find that God has been working in your life all along.

May you accept his abundant gifts with open arms, and then you'll share the joy I feel in rising one more day to live out the most exciting victory a man or woman can ever experience: total surrender to Jesus Christ as Lord.

Acknowledgments

For many years my wife Chris and I have shared our story at couples' events across the country. With each new job as a football coach and new move as a family, more friends, more stories, and more lessons of life were added to our saga. Again and again we were told, "You guys really need to write a book." Again and again we said, "Don't think so." "Not yet." "Maybe one day."

Then one fall day in 2002, as I left a gathering of the Tuesday Morning Quarterback Club men's study that I led at Brentwood Baptist Church, my good friend and pastor Mike Glenn stopped me in the hallway. He asked me when I was going to write that book and put our story in print. When I hesitated—less than enthusiastic—he confronted me bluntly: "I thought you cared about lost men. They need to hear your story. They need to know the truth of God's plan for their lives." I was taken back by his directness and convicted by his challenge. While I knew it was time to share what God had given me, I had no idea what this process would entail. Were it not for the people I wish to acknowledge here, "the book" would still be a far off vision. To them, and others who encouraged me along the way, I will always be grateful.

First, to Valerie Summers with William Morris Agency, who saw the potential my story had to encourage others and had the enthusiasm and skill to convince a publisher.

To Rob Suggs, who patiently listened to my story, heard my heart and worked endless hours to express all that I hoped to convey.

To the professional and caring publishing team at W Publishing Group, including Greg Daniel and Thom Chittom, who guided this rookie through the often challenging process of putting my life in print.

To all the players, coaches, and teams I had the privilege to work with on both the collegiate level and in the NFL, and with whom I shared some great victories and some life-changing defeats.

To the players, coaches, and families of the 2002 State Championship Brentwood Bruins, who encouraged and inspired me in the greatest coaching job I ever had.

To the United States Marine Corps that taught me invaluable lessons of leadership, discipline, and sacrifice, and to the men I served with in Vietnam who lived them out.

To the men of Brentwood Baptist Church, Brentwood, Tennessee, and the Wesleyan Church in Hamburg, New York, especially the "New York Nine" that convinced me that my story could make a difference.

To my spiritual teachers: Charles Stanley, Mike Glenn, Gene Heacock, Larry Thrailkill, and Raymond Berry. They showed me with their wisdom and their lives the purpose to which God calls each of us on this earth.

To John and Barbara White, my dear friends, whose prayers and love for Chris and me have embraced and encouraged us for over thirty years.

To the staff and volunteers of FCA, my new team, who inspire me daily with their faith, dedication, and commitment to the mission of sharing the love of Christ to coaches and athletes across America.

To my parents Bill and Bettie Steckel who taught me the importance of hard work, loyalty, and integrity.

To my in-laws Gene and Betty Pickett who taught me that love, laughter, and devotion make a life-long partnership a blessing.

To my sister Aleita and my brother Dave, whose friendships I cherish.

To my loyal and loving friend Jack Medford who reached out to me as an unsure, walk-on freshman football player at Kansas University and whose friendship has never waivered.

To my children Christian, Lesley, and Luke who allowed me to share some of their stories, and have brought me immeasurable joy and pride as their dad.

To my best friend and forever–partner Chris. She knows this story is our story, and it would never have been told without her contribution at my side.

And finally and most importantly, my abundant gratitude to my Lord and Savior Jesus Christ, who, with patience and forgiveness, set my life on track to intimacy with him, and gave me an understanding of the purpose to which he's called me.